The *Spiritual* Rules of Engagement

Kabbalah Publishing is a registered DBA of
The Kabbalah Centre International, Inc.

For further information:

The Kabbalah Centre
155 E. 48th St., New York, NY 10017
1062 S. Robertson Blvd., Los Angeles, CA 90035

1.800.Kabbalah www.kabbalah.com

First Edition
February 2008
Printed in Canada
ISBN10: 1-57189-592-2
ISBN13: 978-1-57189-592-9

Design: HL Design (Hyun Min Lee) www.hldesignco.com

The

Spiritual

Rules of

Engagement

How Kabbalah Can Help Your Soul Mate Find You

Yehuda Berg

DEDICATION

This book is dedicated to those people who seek out the spiritual truths and who challenge themselves every day to be more so that they can attract their soul mate:

And to those who desire their soul mate so that they can do more.

Ashton'and Demi, I admire your courage.

I love you and support you always.

ACKNOWLEDGMENTS

To the people who make my life better each and every day—my parents, the Rav and Karen, my brother Michael, my wife Michal and our children—and to those who are such an important part of revealing this wisdom through their gifts and support: Stephanie Schottel, Peter Guzzardi, Hyun Min Lee, and Phyllis Henrici. Thank you all.

TABLE OF CONTENTS

Introduction:

Finding Mr. Right

B efore we begin this kabbalistic approach to attracting your soul mate, you need to know two vital kabbalistic principles, for these hold the key to everything you want from your romantic life.

First, contrary to popular belief, opposites do not attract. This is a fallacy. A myth. It's an illusion of the highest order, an illusion that even science does not yet fully see through. Consider two magnets that attract via the seemingly opposite positive and negative (north and south) poles—this, however, is not really what's happening on a deeper level of reality. Kabbalistic wisdom tells us that there is a deeper truth: *Like attracts like* and opposites repel.

Now let's look at the second kabbalistic principle by posing a question:

> *If a good woman marries an evil man and an*
> *evil woman marries a good man, how do you*
> *think these two relationships work out?*

If you assume that good wins out in both cases—that the good man transforms the evil woman, and the good woman transforms the evil man—you're completely wrong. Unquestionably, this is not the case. Who wins out in both cases? Kabbalah says unequivocally: the woman.

By the time you complete this book, you will understand the reasons why opposites do not attract and why a woman is key to a loving and soulful relationship. Once you master these two principles, all the Spiritual Rules of Engagement will make perfect sense, and you will know how to use them to help you achieve everything your heart—and soul—desire.

You're out with the girls for a night on the town. You see a guy who catches your eye. Do you make the first move, or wait for him to do so?

Your boyfriend (or husband) of five years has stopped paying as much attention to you as he used to. You feel ignored and don't know how to bring excitement back into the relationship. Where do you go from here?

You have no problems finding men, but the men you bring home don't seem to stick around long. They always seem to jump ship before the relationship ever leaves port. What gives?

If you have ever stepped out on the playing field of relationships, you have undoubtedly felt frustration. After going out with various men, you may have become discouraged—or even lost all hope of meeting the right guy. Or it may be that despite doing everything right—everything you have been taught, that is—your relationships with men never result in a long-term commitment, let alone marriage. Perhaps you have met someone special, but you're discovering that making that relationship work feels like, well, work—and a whole lot of it. You may be worrying about being alone forever or about being abandoned by the man currently in your life. You may have an inkling of how relationships are supposed to unfold, based on how you saw your parents interact, what you have seen in movies, and the anecdotes you hear from your friends. But despite any knowledge you may have acquired on the subject, you feel as if you are pretty much shooting in the dark on this whole relationship thing.

Whether you have been around the relationship block a few times or are just joining the game, if you aspire to find a lasting partnership rooted in spiritual fulfillment, this book is for you. Not only is this book written for you, it is really all *about* you. That's because the development of any relationship you enter into with a man rests upon *you*—

your motives, your consciousness, your actions. In fact, the reason you feel discouraged by a relationship—or the lack thereof—in your life is because you do not yet recognize the phenomenal power that resides inside you.

When you fail to see this power, you are left feeling empty and frustrated, lonely and abandoned. This book will not only help you discover that power within, but will show you how to use it to your ultimate advantage. Yes, finding the right man and sustaining a lifelong partnership rests entirely in your hands. You—the woman—are in control, and throughout this book, I'll explain exactly why, from a kabbalistic perspective, this is always the case.

Just so you know up front, I won't be dishing out dating tips. There are plenty of books out there that you can pick up if you are simply looking for a few hints on how to meet a man, and some of those books might even work. But if you aim not just to find a great man but to keep him for the long haul, there are universal spiritual rules that you need to learn. These universal spiritual laws, which kabbalists have written about for centuries, will provide you with a surprisingly simple and practical approach to creating lasting fulfillment in a loving partnership.

I know some of you out there are thinking: *But I have a unique situation*, or *my man is different*. But I've never come across a total anomaly when it comes to relationships—not one. Despite the fact that people will offer me all sorts of reasons why their situation doesn't conform to the norm, there are no exceptions. That's because we are talking about Universal Laws, like the Law of Gravity, that apply to everyone; no one is immune to their effects. These universal spiritual laws, by their very nature, level the playing field. No one is at an advantage—or disadvantage—when it comes to forging a lasting, loving relationship.

So it's time to leave your excuses, your justifications, and your defense mechanisms at the door, and open yourself to an entirely different way of understanding the role of man and woman in a relationship. Once you understand the precise role you are meant to play, not only will the simplicity of it blow your mind, but this knowledge will completely transform your relationship with a man.

THE SOUL VERSUS THE INTELLECT

One of the things that I love about Kabbalah is that it's not about right and wrong. Kabbalah is not about morality, ethics, or religion. Kabbalah is about learning how to receive unending fulfillment; this is the only reason why we decide to make changes in our lives. At first glance, this might appear self-centered, but in truth, it is anything but. Why? As you will discover in these pages, the only way to receive unending fulfillment is by treating others with unconditional kindness and love.

According to Kabbalah, loving behavior is not simply practiced for its own sake; it is the secret to receiving everything that *you* want out of life. You see, the problem with moral standards and ethics is that they don't offer any personal reward, for one reason: God created the world with its diverse people to provide us with the opportunity to receive and experience the greatest pleasure and happiness possible. We achieve this through our relationships with others. Therefore, seeking happiness and experiencing pleasure is how we express the will of the Creator.

According to Kabbalah, merely serving an ideal will inevitably leave the individual unfulfilled and lacking. Why? The satisfaction derived from serving an idea is intellectual. Intellectual satisfaction will never completely fulfill a human being. Kabbalah tells us that when we get right down to the most fundamental level, human beings seek absolute fulfillment and pleasure on the level of the human soul. The soul constantly seeks to be filled with spiritual Light and energy. Therefore, learning how to achieve this kind of soul-level fulfillment is the sole purpose (pun intended) behind mastering the wisdom of the ancient kabbalists.

THE ORIGIN OF RELATIONSHIPS

Kabbalah is about being effective in this life. Simply put, this book is about how to be effective in relationships with men. Applying the specific insights of Kabbalah to your relationship is like finding a detailed roadmap after years of flying blind. The Universe is handing you, smart woman that you are, a map based on 2000 years of remarkably timely wisdom to help you successfully navigate your love relationship. As you and I both know, most men don't readily ask for directions, so it is up to you. This is it. The power is in your hands.

THE MAP

Kabbalah is the ultimate GPS technology for finding the right partner and reaching your destination of a soul mate relationship via the most efficient route. All romantic relationships are actually a microcosm of one particular relationship that took place many eons ago. All the romantic relationships of humankind are branches from that one root, that one *original* seed that came into existence quite some time ago. Let's call it the *Very First Relationship*.

To understand the dynamic underlying every human connection, we must grasp the nature of this original, archetypal relationship. Let's now rewind billions of years to discover the origins of romance, relationships, and a true soul connection.

MEET MR. RIGHT

Before our current physical reality erupted into existence (an event dubbed the Big Bang by science), there was a single, unending Force, a Divine Emanation. Let's call this Divine Force, *Mr. Right*. The essential impulse of this Divine Force was the *Desire to Share*—endlessly. Mr. Right had *everything* to give, but no one to give it to. So Mr. Right created the ultimate *receiver*, a glorious being who would become the recipient of the unconditional love, joy, and fulfillment that Mr. Right was prepared to share unceasingly.

In the lexicon of Kabbalah, this being of *receiving* is called a *Vessel*. Its very nature was to accept and delight in everything that Mr. Right was imparting. This is the birthplace of the male and female principles.

Before we go any further, I want to clear up a bit of potential confusion. Mr. Right's name has no connection whatsoever with right and wrong. You may be surprised to learn that it is, however, directly related to direction—as in *right* and *left*. Allow me to explain.

Kabbalists tell us that the Bible is written in highly coded language, which has many layers of hidden meaning. The Bible makes frequent reference to the right side of God and the left side of God. The *Zohar*, the most important source of kabbalistic wisdom, also employs the concepts of right and left in numerous passages. Let's think about this for a moment. God is said to be Infinite. If that's the case, God cannot have a right or a left side. That would be impossible since God is everywhere, filling all eternity. By cracking this code of right and left, we can begin to understand the secret behind a lasting, soul mate relationship.

DECIPHERING RIGHT AND LEFT

The concept of *right* actually refers to the male principle: the flowing, outward emanation of Divine Energy that kabbalists have termed the *Light*. The concept of left refers to the female principle: the receiving entity that acts as the recipient of the energy flowing from the *right*. Kabbalists designate the left as *Vessel*.

So Mr. Right is really a force of Light, or Divine Pleasure. This flowing, blissful Light seeks only to fulfill and enrich. The Vessel (the left) is the female principle, created for the sole purpose of accepting and experiencing the pleasure that is the flowing Light.

In short, right and left are really Sharing (+) and Receiving (–), or Cause and Effect.

The *Zohar* tells us that the Light created the Vessel so that that two could be united in a kind of Divine Matrimony— or Holy connection—for all eternity. This is the reason why the Light created the Vessel in the first place.

We now have what appears to be all the ingredients for a perfect relationship: right and left connected, male and female unified as a whole, *fulfillment* and *desire* integrated as one.

So what happened? From this perfect state, how did we arrive at the world we live in today?

A FUNNY THING HAPPENED ON THE WAY TO THE WEDDING

We could view the initial creation of the Vessel as an engagement, a sort of trial period before a full commitment. Despite this seemingly perfect match of right and left, of sharing and receiving, of Light and Vessel, the engagement was suddenly broken off. *Why* this engagement was broken is the most significant question in all of kabbalistic wisdom. Let's examine this issue by returning to the two kabbalistic principles discussed at the outset of this book:

- *Like attracts like; opposites repel.*
- *A woman is responsible for the success of a relationship.*

THE LAW OF ATTRACTION

There is one all-important law that operates in the spiritual realm. It is called the Law of Attraction. Many have attempted to write about the *Law of Attraction*; however, from the kabbalistic viewpoint, they have completely misunderstood its meaning. Without a true understanding of this law, our relationships will fail to improve in a lasting way.

Thankfully, Kabbalah revealed the meaning of the Law of Attraction thousands of years ago. In a nutshell, this law states that when two entities are similar, they are considered close. Alternatively, the more dissimilar they are, the greater the distance that opens up between them.

Now let's think about this for a moment. The Light (+) and the Vessel (−), or right and left, are actually *opposite* in nature. This is why the engagement was broken off. The Light and the Vessel (or Soul), which was originally created to receive the Light, were separated from one another by virtue of their opposite forms.

At this juncture, I must make a minor digression to introduce a word that is often misunderstood by most people. The word is *consciousness*.

Consciousness is not just a passive state; it is actually a force. It is an intelligent form of energy that behaves according to its own innate intelligence. In other words, the behavior of the energy and its consciousness are one and the same thing. The Light is a force of consciousness whose intelligence is positive sharing, which is why the Light expands and imparts, banishing darkness by its very presence.

The Vessel, on the other hand, is a force of consciousness whose sole nature is receiving. Because these two forms of consciousness are so totally dissimilar, they disconnected from one another countless years ago, and a vast expanse of space separated them.

A SOLUTION

Fortunately, this broken engagement is not a permanent condition. You see, the Light possessed infinite wisdom, so the Light foresaw the separation that would occur as a result of the Law of Attraction. Therefore, when the Light created the Vessel, the Light included within the Vessel a solution to the problem posed by the law that *like attracts like; opposites repel.* What was this solution?

The Light imbued the Vessel (Soul) with an aspect of the Light itself. Now please pay close attention to this next idea because all the problems a woman faces in life are directly tied to it.

THE PROBLEM AND A DEFINITION OF RECEIVING

As long as a woman receives, she remains disconnected from the Light because her nature is in opposition to the nature of the Light. This leads to the question: How does Kabbalah define the word *receiving*?

Simply put, receiving takes place when you experience pleasure as a result of an influence from *outside* of you, or in other words, when an external entity—a man or a situation—is the Cause of your happiness. In such a case, you are merely an *Effect*, a passive receiver. As long as a woman looks to some external force—a man, her career, a material possession, or any kind of external relationship—to make her happy, this is considered to be receiving and will cause disconnection from the Light.

This is why looking for approval from others, because you're feeling empty inside, is such a fruitless strategy. The very act of looking outside yourself disconnects you from the Light, which only makes you feel emptier. You're caught up in a vicious cycle.

So to summarize, the Law of Attraction tells us that when you receive, you disconnect from the Light.

This next part can be a bit confusing, so pay especially close attention.

WHERE IS THE LIGHT?

We talked about how the original Light and the creation of the Vessel (Soul) are the sources of male and female energy. However, a man is not the Light that I am referring to here when I say there is separation and distance between you (the Vessel) and the Light. This is where women who look to men as the source of their happiness and fulfillment go wrong.

A man (I don't care how handsome, rich, or spiritual he may be) is not the original Male Principle or Mr. Right (Light) that we talked about earlier. The original Light that shone before the Creation of the Universe, the Divine

17

Radiance that is the source of all pleasure and fulfillment—*this is the Light* that you separate yourself from when you receive. So where do men fit into all of this? What role do they play in the cosmic scheme of things? I'll explain momentarily.

But first, we must ask these all-important questions: Where does this original Divine Light reside? And if the Light is endless, why can't we see it all the time?

Kabbalah tells us that the world around us—the reality that we experience through our five senses—represents a mere 1 Percent of true reality. The remaining 99 Percent is hidden from ordinary human perception. The unseen 99 Percent Realm is where the Light is. Let's now find out precisely where this is.

THERE'S NO PLACE LIKE HOME

The Light that occupies the 99 Percent Realm is not somewhere up in the sky, or high on a mountaintop, or deep in outer space, or even in some supernal realm called Heaven. That is the stuff of myth. The true Light, the realm where the original Light and Vessel reside, is actually deep within us. I am not waxing poetic when I say this. On the contrary, I am waxing *geographic*. In other words, I am giving you the road map, the actual GPS coordinates for finding the true Light and the 99 Percent Realm.

Far below the gray matter that makes up the human brain, deep within the molecules and atoms and sub-atomic particles, far below all the constituent particles (still to be discovered by science) that give rise to protons, electrons, leptons and quarks, you will eventually reach an infinite sea of energy. This unending pool of Divine Power is the source of all that is. This is the wellspring of Creation. This is the *real* Heaven. This is the limitless realm of the luminous consciousness of Divine Light, otherwise known as the 99 Percent Reality.

Unfortunately, humankind has always cast its eyes towards the sky when searching for Heaven or seeking out the Creator. Wrong direction. Beyond the sky is nothing but the empty vacuum of deep space. My friends, that is not Heaven. Heaven is warm, luminous, overflowing with energy, and infinitely blissful. We have sought out every possible external site, but no matter where we have looked, Heaven and God were nowhere to be found. Perhaps it is time we looked in a new direction: *within*.

Even science is starting to discover that an infinite ocean of energy (scientists call it *Zero Point Energy*) exists at the most fundamental level of reality deep beyond the sub-atomic realm. This is why spiritual teachings tell us to look *within* when searching for the Divine. Each of us is either connected to—or disconnected from—this Infinite Realm by virtue of our consciousness, that is, through our thoughts and subsequent behavior. It is our thoughts—and the behavior that our thoughts compel—that determine whether or not we connect to or separate from this luminous Energy.

CONNECTING TO THE DIVINE

When you do make contact with your inner Light, that's when the magic happens. Waves of Light and a rippling surge of energy fill your mind, your body, and your soul. This is bliss. This is complete contentment. And it includes every other joyful, positive feeling you've ever experienced. Whenever you've experienced *enduring* happiness—*enduring* being the key word here—it's because you made contact with this inner dimension of Divinity. As we will explore shortly, every wonderful idea, inspiration, creative thought, or premonition that emerges in your mind originates from this inner 99 Percent Reality. When everything goes right in your life, you're connected. When things go wrong, space separates you from this 99 Percent Source. Life is as simple as that.

But here's the problem most women face. They look to the outside world for their happiness, which puts them into a receiving mode, which means they're disconnected from the hidden 99 Percent Realm. Bingo! You've just discovered the underlying cause behind all the loneliness, discontent, and depression in the world. The fact is the world around you can never change until the world inside you changes first. It's the simple rule of Cause and Effect. Our 1 Percent World is an Effect. The hidden reality of the 99 Percent is the true Cause. You change your life in the 1 Percent World around you by making a change inside you at the level of the Cause.

True reality exists within—inside your mind, your consciousness, your soul. The outside world is merely a reflection, a dream-like mirror image of your inner state of consciousness and being. The outside world brings you exactly the same degree of Light as you have connected to internally. Ergo, the more you ignore the Light within and seek happiness from outside influences (even if he is a hunk with an MBA), the emptier and more frustrating your life becomes.

Life is all about knowing *how to engage*—as in connect— at the most basic level of reality to the spiritual energy deep within you. The Spiritual Rules of Engagement are all about allowing the Vessel (you) to reengage the Light. As you increase your connection to the Source of all Goodness, your true soul mate moves closer to your life. It's in *your* hands, ladies. It always has been.

IT'S ALL ABOUT THE SPACE

So it turns out that life is ridiculously simple (note that I didn't say easy). It's all about eliminating the space and distance that separates us from the Light. But because the meaning of life was hidden from us for some 20 centuries, we have managed to make our lives incredibly complicated. Now, however, we hold in our hands the ultimate treasure map, the path to the true nature of reality and the source of all happiness. It gets even better: The moment we begin living our lives in accordance with the Law of Attraction, seeking the Light within *first*, our everyday lives begin to undergo genuine and lasting change.

Your life, from this point forward, should only be about removing the space that you created through all your years of receiving and of living reactively. As you do this, you'll attract into your life your true soul mate (and every other kind of happiness) in direct proportion to your effort. So how, then, does one remove this space?

The secret for removing this space is found in the Divine DNA that you inherited from the Light.

PEOPLE WHO NEED PEOPLE

There are certain people in this world who can make you happy—*temporarily*. There are also people who can bring you *unending* happiness for all eternity. Likewise, there are people in this world whom *you* can make happy temporarily, while there are others whom only *you* can fill with joy forever.

The only reason we are not overwhelmingly happy is because we have not yet found the right people in our lives. We have not built the right relationships—in business, socially, and, most of all, romantically.

Make no mistake, nothing of a material nature will ever make us happy over the long term, despite what our self-centered, egocentric impulses might tell us. Only relationships with other people can bring us authentic happiness and true fulfillment. Our families, our friends, our spouses, and our colleagues hold the key to happiness—*but not in a reactive, receiving fashion where they become the Cause and we are just the Effect.* We have to master the technique for attracting the right people into our lives by virtue of our connection to the Light within ourselves. This connection must take place first. Connecting to the Light is the indisputable Cause of all Causes; then, and only then, will the Universe align itself so that the right people automatically enter our lives.

Life is all about relationships. The rest of the physical world is merely a distraction. The iPod, the Beemer, the 60" plasma TV, the 4000-square-foot house, the Hermes scarf, Chanel perfume, the Prada handbag, the Jimmy Choo shoes: These provide only temporary gratification. This gratification is not real Light. It's more akin to the sparkle from a long fuse attached to a stick of dynamite.

It is human relationships that provide us with the opportunity to fill our souls with genuine Light and lasting joy.

24

And we achieve these perfect, happy relationships by *first* establishing and building the most important relationship in all of human existence—the relationship between ourselves, our souls, and the glorious Light illuminating the Divine 99 Percent Reality.

PERCEIVING THE WORLD THROUGH THE EYES OF THE SOUL

The strength of our connection to the Light within us affects how we perceive the world around us and how that world unfolds in our personal life. A story that took place in the 1940s offers us an example of this important idea.

Just prior to World War II, a young couple living in Krakow, Poland, was very much in love, so they got engaged. After the war broke out, the Nazis sent the two of them to separate concentration camps. Somehow, they both managed to survive those horrific years and were eventually liberated by the Allies. Shortly after, the man was in a food line with hundreds of other survivors when he spotted a woman in another food line. His heart began racing, his eyes welled up with tears, and he ran over to her, calling out her name.

It was his fiancée. Needless to say, the two were over-joyed beyond words.

The couple went for a long walk to catch up on all those lost and painful years. Eventually, they came upon an empty house. The girl needed to go to the bathroom, so they went inside. Her fiancé became quite concerned when, after a long time, she still hadn't come out of the bathroom. He went and knocked on the door to see if she was okay. There was no reply. Then he heard sobs. He banged on the door and begged her to open it. She finally did.

He asked her why she was crying, why she refused to come out of the bathroom. She wiped away her tears and told him that this was the first time she had seen herself in a mirror in many years. She was aghast at the sight of her-self—all skin and bones, gaunt, pale, and sickly. How could he possibly still love her? The young man held her tightly and said, "Right now, you are the most beautiful woman in the world to me."

At first, she couldn't understand why. He explained that he hadn't even noticed how she looked physically when he first saw her in the food line. Instead, he saw her soul shining, her Light and energy radiating from the very essence of her being. That was how he had first recognized her.

Unfortunately, it often takes great suffering before human beings become open to seeing the soul rather than merely the 1 Percent Illusion. When we connect to the Light within ourselves by not reacting to external influences and the physical 1 Percent World around us, we raise our self-esteem and fill our internal Vessel with Light. Then everything we perceive will be filled with goodness and Light.

During the remainder of this book, we will learn *how* to connect, in a very practical way, to the 99 Percent inside of us. Kabbalists have provided us with constructive tools and powerful techniques that allow us to access and connect to Divine Consciousness, to the blazing endless Light that radiates *everything* we seek from life.

In addition, we will find out how a woman can stop *receiving* so that she may re-connect to the Light and, in turn, allow the Universe to oblige her true soul mate to find his way into her life.

THE POWERFUL WORLD OF THE 99 PERCENT

Where does all of this Light that inhabits the 99 Percent come from? Like all things wonderful, the Light comes from the Creator. In Kabbalah, we don't pretend to understand God entirely. But we do understand a little bit about the power of the Creator's energy. We understand God in much the same way as we understand the sun. Humankind owes its existence to the sun. Without the sun, we die. But we know that if we get too close to the sun, we'll be incinerated. It is the *rays* of the sun that give us life. It is this lustrous *emanation* that supplies mankind and the entire Earth with what we need, not the blazing solar furnace itself.

The Light works the same way. The Light is the energy that the Creator shares with all of the souls of humanity. It is what powers the human immune system and makes the heart beat. It is what makes a flower grow and a baby smile. It's nothing but unadulterated goodness, the ultimate blessing bestowed upon each of us—continuously, without disruption, for all of eternity.

Other spiritual systems assign different names to it, but we are all talking about the same loving Divine Force of energy that emanates from the Creator. Each and every one of us knows this energy intimately because we've all experienced its awesome affects. When we recall a moment when we felt immense joy, well-being, abundance, gratitude, or unshakeable peace of mind, we are recalling an experience with the Light.

The Light is raw love—pure devotion, free of judgment or criticism, a manifestation of what Kabbalah calls the World of 99 Percent, the spiritual realm of the soul. The 99 Percent Realm is the realm of spiritual growth and transformation with the singular purpose of receiving lasting fulfillment. Kabbalah is the study of how to receive and experience the Light of the Creator in our lives right now. In fact, the word *Kabbalah* means *receiving*. Paradoxically, learning how *not to receive* turns out to be one of the very best strategies for receiving the Light.

JUST PART OF THE BIG PICTURE

Inherent in its very name is the fact that the 99 Percent Realm is not the entire picture. If it were, your physical body and these pages you are reading would simply not exist. The 99 Percent Realm exists simultaneously with the

1 Percent Illusionary Realm, which is the world we perceive with our senses: It is the world we see, smell, taste, touch, and hear. But that's not all. The 1 Percent also includes what we think and what we feel.

Surprised? Most people think of thoughts and feelings as something spiritual, but they're not. Why not? Because feelings don't represent the deeper reality of a situation. Just because you feel something doesn't mean it's true. This is not to say that you should deny or ignore the feelings you are having. Not at all. Feelings are important sources of information, but because they are part and parcel of the physical world, they are part of the 1 Percent Reality.

So how does this play out in your our search for worthwhile relationships? The 1 Percent manifests itself in thoughts like these:

- *He's an attractive man; maybe I should go for it.*
- *We've been dating for a while. It's time to move to the next level.*
- *I'm almost 30. It's about time for me to get married. It would make my parents happy if I found someone.*

These are all 1 Percent reasons. Can you guess why? It's because these thoughts are rooted in fear and uncertainty, which do not come from the Light and the 99 Percent World. More importantly, these reasons are based on the premise of you *receiving*, of you being the Effect instead of being the Cause. Any kind of reaction is considered to be an act of receiving, which creates space between you and the Light. Reactions are not good. Henceforth, our kabbalistic definition for *receiving* has now been officially expanded to include any and all kinds of *reactive behavior*.

By now, it should become clear that everything you've been doing thus far in the 1 Percent World has been pretty much a reaction, an Effect, an act of receiving. And this is why the 1 Percent World—and your life—are so distanced from the 99 Percent.

The question that you have to ask yourself is this: Do I want 1 Percent of a man or do I want the whole kit and caboodle, body and soul? If you choose the 1 Percent Man, you are making yourself the ultimate Effect, handing over all control to your male counterpart. This can only lead you to disconnection and darkness.

My guess is that if you are still reading this book, you have intuitively concluded that 1 Percent is simply not enough. You are ready for a relationship that delivers the real goods—fulfillment on both the physical and the soul level.

The 1 Percent World offers immediate gratification. It's like flirting: His attention feels good in the moment, and you don't want to spend an evening alone. You are reacting to the fear of being alone. You are reacting to the impulse of needing attention (energy) from someone outside yourself. Consequently, according to the Law of the Attraction, your reacting is receiving and thus it disconnects you from the 99 Percent. The pleasure derived from flirting quickly evaporates, leaving you even hungrier for attention and energy.

The 99 Percent, on the other hand, represents long-term commitment and lasting fulfillment. If the 1 Percent is a one-night stand, the 99 Percent is the happily-every-after. If the 1 Percent is *Mr. Hottie now*, the 99 Percent is your soul mate forevermore.

Yes, your soul mate! It's a term that gets thrown around pretty liberally these days. Your soul mate is your heart's desire, your kindred spirit, your one true love, right? Sure, but what does all of that really mean? According to Kabbalah, the term "soul mate" has a significance that goes far beyond popular interpretation. Which takes us to a profound question: *Where do men fit into the cosmic scheme of things?*

To find out, we must travel back once again to the beginning of all beginnings.

OUR OTHER HALF

As we discussed earlier, in the beginning before the physical Universe existed, there was endless Light. There was nothing else. And this was the problem. The Light wanted to share the infinite happiness that It embodied, but there was nothing to share it with. So the Light created what kabbalists called the Original Vessel, or the Original Soul. This Vessel, or Soul, was created from the Light, so it contained the very same DNA as the Light itself. If the Light was liquid glass, for example, imagine cooling some of that liquid and sculpting it into the shape of a jar. The jar is a vessel, but the jar is also made out of glass. So the jar has two aspects: the jar itself and the material from which it is made.

The Original Vessel was a container (the female energy) but it was made out of Light (male energy). This is how both male and female energy came to exist in our universe.

Here we also discover the mystery behind the biblical characters of Adam and Eve. Contrary to popular belief, Adam and Eve were not two people inhabiting some mythical garden. Adam and Eve refer to the one Original Vessel and its dual aspect of male and female forces.

This one Vessel was separated from the Light because its nature of receiving was dissimilar to the giving nature of the Light. In other words, *receiving* is the dominant trait of the Vessel. The secondary, less important feature of the Vessel is the substance that it is made of: Light. Because the Vessel's dominant nature is *receiving*, it became distanced from the Light, separated by space. The space created by this opposite nature of the Vessel gave rise to the Big Bang (the birth of literal space) and to our own lives. This, by the way, is why mankind finds itself so far from the Light, so far from a world of pure joy and peace.

However, there is a solution to the plight in which we find ourselves. And the solution to this condition of disconnection and space connects directly to the idea of soul mates. So let's call it a *So(u)lution* instead of a *solution*.

As long as the Vessel continued to receive, it would remain far away from the Light. So the Vessel did something rather spectacular. It stopped receiving, causing itself to shatter in the process. Its male and female aspects tore apart from one another and shattered once more, scattering into the vacuum of empty space (our Universe). This is the origin of the proton (male) and the electron (female) forces that comprise the atom, the building block of all the physical matter that exists. Our entire Universe is, in fact, made up of fragments from the Original Vessel.

What does all this have to do with soul mates? Absolutely everything. Every soul that comes into this world instinctively yearns for the other half of its being that was torn away by the act of shattering of the Original Vessel. Every man has a missing aspect of his soul that is female, and every woman has a missing aspect of her soul that is male. This missing aspect is our own soul's mate.

So a soul mate is not just a myth or a trendy term. Finding one's soul mate is the innate desire of every person on the planet. It's the path to true fulfillment. It's the destiny of every man and woman in this world. And if our soul mate doesn't show up in this lifetime, it will happen in the next—or in the one after that. You see, each of us is reborn over and over again until such time as we reunite with our true soul mate.

> *When a man is new—that is, he is in this world for the first time—his soul mate is born with him, as known, and when the time comes for him to marry her, he finds her immediately without any trouble. But if that man committed a sin and had to incarnate because of it, his soul mate is caused to reincarnate with him for his benefit. When the time comes for this man to marry her, he does not find her immediately, but only after much trouble, for since he incarnated for some iniquity, some denounce him Above and wish to withhold her from him, and cause fights between them. This is why it has been said that it is as hard to unite them as it is to split the Red Sea,*

—Writings of Rav Isaac Luria, *Gates of Reincarnation*, 20th Introduction

This reunification with our soul mate is vitally important and can only take place when we first connect to the Divine Light within ourselves, as we learned earlier on. This has cosmic significance for the following reason.

REPAIRING CREATION

Because it received, the Vessel separated from the Light. When it shattered into pieces, a new opportunity became possible—the opportunity to share. When human beings (the shattered fragments of the Original Soul) transform from receivers into sharers, from takers into givers, we repair that fundamental rift of Creation: We remove the space that erupted into existence when the Light created the Original receiving Vessel. This is the incalculable power of soul mates.

There's a notion going around that the desire for a soul mate is primarily a woman's yearning. Don't be fooled by this nonsense. Men have an equally powerful yearning for a soul mate. Why? Because we all long to find our other half and thus to complete ourselves. In fact, according to Kabbalah, we work for lifetimes—to have the opportunity to reunite with that part of us that has been with us spiritually from the beginning.

We've all met men or women who say, "But I don't want to settle down. I don't want to get married." How does that reconcile with the kabbalistic principle that we all crave our soul mate? This leads us to what I consider to be the most brilliant deception in all of human history.

THE DECEPTION

This deception is the reason why women keep receiving, keep living reactively, keep feeling like victims of external circumstances—even when they know better. This deception is also the reason why men settle for a quick fling or try to achieve as many sexual conquests as possible, even though in their heart of hearts, they seek their true soul mate as well.

For some reason, men and women are not in touch with their true inner selves. Why not? What kind of deception is taking place? Who is deceiving whom?

THE JEALOUS, DEVIOUS FRIEND

Did this ever happen to you or to someone you know? You had a boyfriend. Or a husband. And one of your friends was insanely jealous of your relationship. So this "friend" did everything in his or her power to create a rift, a separation between the two of you. Eventually, this "friend's" devious shenanigans may have even caused a break-up.

Well, the same idea is at work in the Universe every day of your life. Except in life, it is not a jealous friend. It is an angel. Seriously. A real angel, but not a heavenly angel with wings. This angel is an actual force of consciousness that resides inside of you. Now before you allow doubt and cynicism to cloud your thinking, hear me out.

The ancient kabbalists described the Big Bang a full 2000 years before modern-day science. The kabbalists realized that clogging of the arteries caused heart disease and strokes approximately 20 centuries before medical science arrived at the same conclusion. The *Zohar* said the Earth was a sphere with seven continents some 1500 years before Columbus set sail. Kabbalists through the millennia have spoken about parallel universes, atoms, the speed of Light, and other scientific truths we now take for granted

39

but that were completely unknown 100 years ago, let alone 2000 years ago. So if the kabbalists managed to get all that right, perhaps we should take a moment to consider their views concerning a distinct force of consciousness that resides within the recesses of the human mind.

In truth, you are already aware of this consciousness. You just didn't know that it is not unique to you. You know those famous battles that go on inside your head? You promise to cut down on chocolate, but then a voice talks you into buying that big chocolate bar! You promise to start working out, and then that other voice undermines your good intentions. You promise not to divulge a secret, and then the infamous second voice talks you into spilling the beans. Every time you do something that you know you shouldn't, you're seeing the second force of consciousness at work.

The ancient kabbalists gave this force a name: the Adversary. And the reason it is called the *Adversary* is because its sole function is to battle you, to pull you away from the Light. Make no mistake: Twenty-four hours a day, this adversarial force tries to create separation between you and the Light within you, just like an insanely jealous friend. Its sole purpose is to disconnect you from the

Source of all Sources by compelling you to behave in a manner that is opposite to the nature of the Light.

By the way, there is one more thing you need to know about this second conscious force. Almost 3400 years ago, the Bible (the Old Testament), said that this entity has one primary attribute—*doubt!* The Adversary uses this quality as a brilliantly shrewd way to ensure its own continued survival. Let me explain.

The closer you get to the Adversary, the more doubt you have about its existence. Why? Doubt and skepticism radiate from the Adversary, making it nearly impossible to recognize its existence in your own mind because the nearer you get to it, the more you believe it doesn't exist. Get it?

You might be wondering why this second voice, this second conscious entity, exists at all. Why would the Creator make our task that much more difficult? It has to do with free will. In other words, if there were no doubt, if there was no force trying to deceive you all day long, you'd find your soul mate in about six seconds. All humankind would achieve infinite happiness in about the same time frame. However, this happiness would not have been earned. It would be a free lunch, a handout. So the Original Vessel (you and I) asked the Creator to create this angelic force to make finding the Light a more difficult, challenging, and thus, worthy task. We've got to earn our soul mates, which makes them even more desirable.

So it is the Adversary that stands between you and your soul mate. It is the Adversary that encourages you every day to *receive* instead of *give*. It is the Adversary that leads you to react to every outside influence so that you never gain control over your life. This is why women so often look outside of themselves for validation, happiness, acceptance and approval. This is why men cannot find the part of themselves that wants to truly earn their soul mate and settle down. The Adversary is pulling our strings, motivating our behavior, while at the same time, blinding men and women to its very existence.

The Adversary, by the way, takes the form of the human ego. All your life, you were convinced that the impulses and urges of the ego belonged to you. They don't. They belong to the Adversary. The deeper longings of the soul are the real, authentic you. Now that you know this, stop and take a moment to introduce yourself to yourself. Your life will never be the same.

All those doubts, anxieties, feelings of being a victim, lone-liness, depression, frustration, worry, fear, envy, anger and sadness—all these were constructed by the Adversary and planted in your rational mind. Letting go of these self-destructive emotions is a difficult task because we are still not sure (there's that doubt again) that the Adversary is real. After all, these emotions feel so authentic, so real. And this is why I call it the greatest deception in human history.

All in all, the Adversary is a clever, formidable obstacle that we must all overcome. But fortunately, it is the *only* obstacle we need to overcome to change our life. How do we do it? We overcome the Adversary one step at a time. It's a gradual process. But each time we do it, our life grows brighter.

Armed with all of this kabbalistic wisdom, we can better understand why people (specifically men) behave the way they do. When people say that they'd prefer to remain single, what they are really revealing is their vast disconnect from the 99 Percent Reality caused by the influence of the Adversary. They are choosing to remain alone because they believe that being with another person poses a much greater risk. Fear and uncertainty have poisoned their understanding of love and relationships. They blame another person instead of the Adversary for their hurt as well as their own disconnection from the Light.

Because they don't know the Spiritual Rules of Engagement, the Universal Laws at work behind the scenes, they go on choosing temporary relationships or no relationships at all, at the expense of a deep interpersonal connection. And they are not alone. Many of you can admit to making this mistake—even those of you who have made it clear that you aspire to meet that special someone. Kabbalah is about unlimited fulfillment, and when we learn to cultivate that in our relationships and reap the Divine benefits, no one would intentionally choose to make a go of life without a partner by his or her side.

But fear ignited by the Adversary can keep us separated from love, joy, and our soul mate. So many of us walk around unaware of the deep motivating force that underlies all of our actions: a fear of not making it, of not finding true love, of not having children, of not manifesting our potential, of not being the person you wish you could be. This fear causes untold amounts of pain. But we do our best to bury it, which protects the very Adversary that is its cause.

Unbeknownst to us (at least until now), fear has remained a driving force in our lives. Instead of being driven by the desire to be effective, we were being propelled by the fear of not being successful. A life motivated by fear and anxiety is sure to be a struggle, while a life motivated by a proactive desire to be effective and connected has Light written all over it.

So how do women become more effective with men? You subscribe to a few Spiritual Rules of Engagement and know that the wisdom to do so already rests inside of you. What are those rules? We'll examine them in detail in a moment, but first we must realize that the ultimate goal of a relationship is *love*. In case you hadn't noticed, a goal is something that we achieve after a lot of hard work; a goal is never achieved at the outset. Let's examine this idea further and discover the basis for a loving relationship so that we can truly comprehend the power underlying the Spiritual Rules of Engagement.

LOVE IS THE REWARD

There is an unusual quote in the Old Testament about the biblical patriarch known as Isaac. Isaac was the son of

Abraham, who was the father of the Israelites, Muslims, and Christians. Isaac married a girl by the name of Rebecca. As the Bible puts it:

"And Isaac brought her into his mother Sarah's tent, and took Rebecca, and she became his wife; and he loved her."
(Genesis 24:67)

In our modern day world, it's usually the other way around, isn't it? We meet, we fall in love, and *then* we marry. Contrary to popular belief, when it comes to the way a true soul mate relationship works, the Bible had it right. True love is not the Cause in the marriage of two people. True love is the Effect. It is the net result of many years of hard work, effort, and, most importantly, spiritual transformation. True love is a reward. It has to be earned by both husband and wife.

The problem today is that couples have it backwards. We've been led to believe that love comes at the outset of a marriage, that love is the reason for getting married. And then we're left scratching our heads after a few months or a few years, wondering where the thrill has gone and why the passion and heat have dissipated from the relationship.

So here's the problem: What people call *love* is actually *need*. Big difference between the two. Ask someone why they love their boyfriend or girlfriend and nine times out of ten, you'll hear answers like:

- *They make me feel loved.*
- *They understand me and accept me for who I am.*
- *They give me space and make me feel secure and safe.*
- *They bring out the best in me.*
- *They care for me and treat me with respect.*

And if they're talking about Jerry McGuire, they'll tell you: *He completes me!*

These are all nice sentiments. But all of these responses, though they might *sound* like definitions for love, are actually no such thing. What is being described here is *need*. In other words, the people offering up these responses are talking about their *own* needs and desires. That is not love. Love is not about *receiving*. Love is not about what you're *getting* from the relationship. Love is only about *giving*. Love is about what you're *putting into* the relationship—unconditionally, without any expectations or desire to receive something back.

Love is never about the *me*. Love is only about the *other person* whom you're sharing with. Pleasure and fulfillment come from the act of sharing with the person you love. You experience *their* happiness. Granted, this is a lofty state of consciousness, but we can all get there if we put in the years of spiritual growth and transformation. And getting there is *supposed* to take time.

All relationships start out as a form of need, as we seek to fulfill our own desires. But if we use the wisdom and power of a spiritual technology like Kabbalah to transform ourselves, we gradually achieve the ability to love the other person unconditionally—and to be loved the same way in return. Both partners derive their own pleasure by devoting themselves to pleasing and fulfilling the other.

In this state, we accept the kindness, care, love, and gifts that our partner bestows upon us because we know that our partner derives so much pleasure from the act of giving. *Now we are receiving for the sake of sharing.* A wonderful circuit of energy has been established, whereby even the act of receiving has been transformed into an act of sharing. It's a powerful dynamic that creates nothing less than miracles and arouses untold Divine pleasure for both partners. But again, this kind of unconditional love is attained only in a true soul mate relationship, and these lofty heights of love are achieved only after years of striving and transforming for the sake of the other person.

LIKE ATTRACTS LIKE

The common denominator at the heart of a soul mate relationship is that *first* both parties have established a bond and connection with the Light within themselves. Remember, at the very heart of reality lies that infinite ocean of Divine energy. When we tap into it, we gain access to unending fulfillment and love. Put simply, the common denominator is that both partners in a soul mate relationship have the common goal of connecting to the Divine Source within. Thus, there is no sense of need and selfish desire in relation to the other person. Each person is secure and fulfilled in themselves, which makes them free to share their goodness with the other—with no strings attached.

On every level, the Law of Attraction (*like attracts like*) is operating. First, the two partners share the identical goal of connecting to the Creator by emulating the nature and behavior of the Light. This is the full expression of *like attracts like*. Second, they are both walking the same spiritual path, nourishing themselves from the same spiritual fountainhead. Once again, *like attracts like*. Their spiritual goals are one and the same. Their understanding of the nature of reality and the ways of the world are the same. And their common goal of sharing happiness unconditionally with the other person, and with the rest of the world, is yet another example of similarity and affinity.

A PLACE FOR OPPOSITE VIEWS

This does not mean both parties in a relationship have to have the same opinions and tastes. *Like attracts like* need only be the *spiritual* basis of a relationship and expresses itself in the *behavior* of one person towards another. Both partners must be identical to the Light in terms of behavior and deeds: behaving with unconditional sharing and caring, expecting nothing in return.

For a relationship to transcend the sum of its parts in other areas of life, opposite views are healthy and much needed. In this regard, the partners can be virtual opposites. Here's an example. Two people are in business together. They share the same goal of success, the same goal of profits, and the same goal of building the business. But one of the partners is a creative marketing type, and the other enjoys accounting and financial matters. These are two very different strengths, but both are crucial to building a business. The creative tension between these opposite poles contributes balance so that the right decisions, strategies, and directions can emerge in any given situation. Both parties allow room for the Light to enter into their relationship and into their business, so the company is aligned with the natural flow of the Universe.

My own parents provide a wonderful example of balance in a relationship. Their own story is so dramatic that it reads like a novel. My father, the Rav, and my mother, Karen, were opposites. Completely. The Rav came from a traditional, intolerant, strict orthodox religious background. My father met his master in the early 1960s and was introduced to the world of Kabbalah, eventually becoming the successor to his teacher, the renowned Rav Yehuda Brandwein. The transformation my father was forced to undergo—from religious to spiritual, from dogmatic rabbi to open-minded kabbalist—was a painful and turbulent process.

My mother, on the other hand, rode a Harley-Davidson. She wore mini-skirts, and her family was strictly secular. My mom was a free spirit who possessed a keen interest in astrology, spirituality, and other esoteric subjects. The story of how my parents came together has been told in many other books. The point that I want to bring out here is that when they started their marriage, my parents shared an interest in Kabbalah and a desire to share Kabbalah and the *Zohar* with the entire world. They possessed the same goal of spiritual transformation and the same goal of removing pain and suffering from the landscape of human civilization. That was the Law of Attraction, of *like attracts like* at work.

But in terms of their backgrounds, upbringing, and personal interests, my parents were polar opposites. In those early years, the Rav was opposed to television and modern culture, one of the few remaining elements of his youth, which was spent in a strict orthodox environment. The Rav refused to allow my mom to watch TV. My mom wouldn't stand for it. She understood that spirituality is not about dogma, narrow-mindedness, and cutting oneself off from the rest of the world. On the contrary, it's about embracing the physical world in order to change it and about bringing a sense of sacredness to everything that one does. In other words, she knew that it wasn't the TV shows that we watched that were the problem. The problem was how we treated one another.

If someone enjoyed watching a trashy TV show but would give you the shirt off his or her back, that was far more important to my mom than someone who resisted watching an R-rated movie out of religious beliefs but was intolerant and disrespectful towards anyone who was different from him or her. So when the Rav refused to allow TV in the house, my mother told the Rav in no uncertain terms that if the TV went out the door, so would the Rav!

The TV stayed.

My mom was once forced to toss a religious piece of clothing that my father wore, a fur hat called a *streimal*, off the balcony of their apartment because the Rav was still stuck in a religious, intolerant mindset on various matters. To my mom, it wasn't the clothes people wore on the outside that mattered, but rather the soul of the individual on the inside.

My mom was also forced to undergo major changes in regard to the kabbalistic practices of the Rav. My mom embraced a whole new challenging world. See what's happening here?

Two opposites come together, through hard, difficult work, change, and growth. But always aiming for the shared goal of spiritual transformation and sharing Light with other people. *Like attracts like* was their underlying foundation.

Both sides in a relationship must work to let go of their negative traits. And both sides must share their positive and often opposite traits and opinions with each other so both views can be embraced. That is the glue that keeps a relationship together. The road will get bumpy and turbulent, heated and stressful, but beneath it all, there will be dignity, respect and a desire to fill the relationship with Light.

The love between the Rav and my mom grew each year. It was a deep, spiritual and unconditional love, earned and nurtured through many long years of striving, change, and most importantly, putting concern for the well-being of other people ahead of their own. I certainly used to see my parents in some heated arguments. But you know what? Those arguments were always about the welfare of other people. Without fail. My parents never argued over their own needs and desires. The arguments were always over the right way to help someone else or how best to deal with and solve someone else's problems. Make no mistake, there were some rip-roaring scream-fests. But their hearts and souls were focused on helping and sharing, not on receiving. My mom said it best: *If you get busy worrying about others, the Light gets busy worrying about you.*

HER OWN WOMAN

The Rav was always larger than life. But my mom never allowed herself to be the proverbial "rabbi's wife," or "the wife of a kabbalist." My mother was her own person. She was Karen. She found her own connection to the Light and stood on her own—with great strength, a deep sense of purpose, and a secure interdependence with the Rav. She was a true partner in the deepest sense of the word, allowing the Rav to manifest all the Light that he was meant to reveal.

Growing up in our household, I witnessed firsthand two people become one spirit, one complete soul. I must say there are no words that I can put to paper that could possibly express my appreciation for the parents with whom I have been blessed. By being in their presence, I have gained some insight into how it was that Isaac met Rebecca, married her, and then loved her.

Once we know and appreciate this order of things (meet, marry, love) when we enter a relationship, we suddenly gain a whole new perspective on the problems and turmoil that can arise during the first few years of the relationship. More importantly, by focusing first on the Light of the Creator, the source of energy within us, we imbue our own life with ever-increasing joy and fulfillment.

EVE AND THE GOLDEN CALF

My mom also helped me understand the role and importance of a woman in today's world. These relate directly to the story of Adam and Eve and the story of Moses and the Golden Calf. For those not familiar with both stories, I promise to keep it simple. Essentially, the traditional story of Adam and Eve tells us that Eve is the one who sinned as a result of listening to the serpent in the Garden of Eden. Eve partook of an apple from the infamous Tree of Knowledge of Good and Evil. The *Zohar* says that this story is a code concealing a much deeper idea. The idea is this: There was One Vessel. Only one. The One Vessel possessed both male and female aspects.

In the tale of Adam and Eve, the serpent is a code for the Adversary, that part of our consciousness that makes us react, that aspect of our rational mind that makes us irrational, selfish, angry, and self-serving. The part of the Vessel that indulged the Adversary was the female aspect, for that is the receiving force. When the Vessel indulges the ego, it becomes an empty Vessel. It remains dark. Thus, when the Vessel broke into two, male separating from female, the female force had a karmic debt to repair.

When the female aspect of the Vessel shattered once more, it created countless souls—all the women destined to walk this planet, each woman bearing a part of that spiritual debt. This is the underlying reason why women in history tended to look to external influences and other people's approval (particularly men) for their Light.

Let us now fast-forward to Moses, Mount Sinai, and the Revelation of the Two Tablets. The *Zohar* tells us that this Revelation was actually a time of full illumination of the Light of the 99 Percent Reality. Moses had connected the 1 Percent physical dimension to the 99 Percent, and thus all darkness—including death itself—was banished from the face of the Earth. So what happened? Where is the Light that shone on Mount Sinai? Why is death part of our lives if it was banished at the time of Mount Sinai?

The short version is this: While Moses was up on the mountain sealing the deal, so to speak, the Israelites panicked. They thought Moses was never going to return. In truth, it was the Adversary deceiving the Israelites, causing them to doubt and filling their heads with all kinds of self-centered fears and worries. All the Israelites had to do to solidify and make permanent this condition of bliss and immortality was to resist the provocations of the Adversary. But they didn't. They made the choice—of their own free will—to listen to their egos.

So the Israelites gathered up all the gold from the 600,000 people camped out at the base of the mountain and they constructed a Golden Calf. This calf was going to act as technological intermediary to connect the Israelites directly to the 99 Percent Realm. Needless to say, it didn't work. Why? Selfishness, impatience, and ego stand in opposition to the Light. Thus, the behavior of the Israelites created a separation from the Light. As a result, death was reborn.

The kabbalists and the ancient biblical writings tell us that the women did not participate in the building of the

Golden Calf. The women knew the Israelite men were shooting themselves in the foot, and they wanted no part of it. The women maintained certainty that Moses was returning, and they made sure not to use their power—not to turn over their internal Vessel to darkness. *This* time, they would *not* react to the external provocations of the Adversary. When women allow their Vessel to be used to reveal darkness they are treated like objects, receiving no respect or dignity. It is in the hands of a woman to decide what her Vessel will be used for: for selfishness, insecurity, and negativity, or for sharing and revealing goodness and Light.

I share this story and insight with you because it was at that precise moment in history at Mount Sinai when all women—past, present, and future—corrected the karmic debt of the Original Vessel. That was the moment when all women completed their job and spiritual work in this physical world because they used their Vessel for what it was intended. That was 3400 years ago. All women have been doing for the last 34 centuries is waiting for men to catch up! A lot of blood has been spilled during this period. When men finally change, this world will be restored to its original state of bliss and immortality.

But it is not just men's fault that they have remained prisoners to their egos, slaves to the Adversary. Women have also been unaware of their own role in the cosmic scheme of things. Their job is to help straighten men out using the Spiritual Rules of Engagement and the wisdom in this book. Know why women are not aware of any of this? Because ego-driven men throughout history kept the teachings of Kabbalah secret. All that ends now. Women are hereby empowered to take their rightful place in this world and to help their men get their act together so that the dawn of a new peaceful world will unfold before our very eyes. Expect and demand nothing less.

With this in mind, we are now ready to explore the Spiritual Rules of Engagement on a practical level.

Rule Number One:

Men are channels for the Light, while women are Vessels for the Light.

The *Spiritual* Rules of Engagement

J ust as the Light of the Creator and the Original Vessel had fundamentally different roles, men and women also have specific functions. But before we discuss these differences, let's talk about the one similarity that binds men and women together: When we are referring to our relationship with the Light, both men and women are Vessels for the Light of the Creator. The Creator designed each of us for the sole purpose of *receiving* His everlasting joy and fulfillment.

But when we look at the relationship between men and women on this earthly plain, the function of our respective Vessels differ. When you understand why this is the case, you will understand why men and women think differently, why we perceive differently, why we behave differently, and why we need to learn to negotiate our relationships with each other differently.

Many authors on the subject of relationships offer good advice based on the accurate assessment that men and women are different. But what they cannot tell you is *why* we are so different. Kabbalah answers this question from a spiritual standpoint, and in the answer lies the key to loving, worthwhile relationships.

So what is the male soul? Think of a pipe, a conduit with the ability to channel Light. This is the structure of the male soul. Energy goes in; energy comes out. At the level of the 1 Percent, or physical level, a man expresses the desire to share his Light as a desire for sex. The energy of the man craves contact with the energy of the woman. We'll talk in more detail about this attraction in our next chapter. For now, you also need to know that on the 99 Percent, or spiritual level, a man wants to share his Light in order to fulfill the Vessel. This is an important distinction.

What men want more than anything in a relationship is the ability to make a woman happy and earn her love.

Did you know that? Maybe not, and guess what? Most men aren't aware of it either because the Adversary (the male ego) tries to keep all men from knowing how simple this is. But the Adversary's efforts at hiding the truth do not make it any less true. The structure of the male channel is to bring Light into the world in order to fulfill and earn a woman's love. That is a man's function, which makes him action–oriented by his very nature. Men are problem-solvers. Men are doers. They have an innate drive to share with others the energy that they are receiving from the Light of the Creator.

Some of you reading this book might be shaking your heads and saying, "My man is definitely not action-oriented." But once you strip away ego, fear, and the confusion of the 1 Percent World in which we live, a man's very essence is to share Light and to do for others.

Women often bear witness to this when they share their problems with a man. How does he usually respond? He wants to fix things, right? You can almost hear the gears in his brain turning as he comes up with the "solution" to your dilemma. He wants to help. He wants to make things better for you. He wants to assist in some way. Why? Because his job is to satisfy, to fulfill.

Unfortunately, this is often misinterpreted as a lack of compassion, care, or listening skills on his part. What you are experiencing, however, is a man sharing (the Light he is receiving) with you in the only way he knows how.

But as you're about to discover, it's the job of the woman to manage and direct that influx of Light. Yes, women are the relationship managers, the Light managers. I'll explain what that means in more detail as we delve deeper into the specific roles of men and women.

YOU ARE THE CEO

One of the fundamental reasons why women are frustrated in relationships is because they don't understand that they run the relationship. For all intents and purposes, you are the chief executive officer of a company called Relationship. Just as you wouldn't leave your company in the hands of a six-year-old while you are on vacation, you shouldn't leave your relationship in the hands of a man. Managing a relationship is not part of a man's skill set. Nor is it a man's role. And if you continue to expect a man to fulfill that role, you will be disappointed again and again.

Now don't get me wrong. There are things that men do well, but managing a relationship with a woman is usually not one of them. So you must be willing to take full responsibility for the relationship or it won't be successful. The power rests with you and the decisions that you make.

A man is a channel, a pipeline for the Light. That's all he is. And his fundamental desire is to please you. As a woman, your role is to honor his desire to please you and to support his role of channeling the energy of the Creator into this world. In other words, he wants to share his Light with you. He wants to cherish you, and your job is to allow that to happen.

When you accept a man's Light into your life, you become responsible for directing that Light. Think of it this way. Let's say that the front door to your apartment needs to be replaced. You call a handyman to come and fix it. The guy arrives and says, "Lady, it's going to be $800 to repair your door. I want the entire amount up front in cash before I can begin work." Are you going to give it to him? Hopefully not, right?

What are you going to do? You might say, "I'll give you $200 now for materials. After you've done the job, if I like the way it looks, I'll pay you the rest." Right? But so many women don't do that in relationships. Metaphorically speaking, many women just go along and pay the full $800 up front, and then wonder why they are left frustrated after a lousy repair.

All too often, women hope for the best when it comes to a relationship with a man, instead of putting their inherent management skills to work. Without effective management of energy, there can be no healthy relationship. This is not to place blame on women in any way, shape or form. This is not a blame game at all. It's simply a matter of women not fully recognizing the extent of their power and of the ability they have to make this world a better place by effectively managing their relationships with men.

What do I mean by managing a relationship? Let's look at one specific example. If there is one mistake many employers make, it is this: They hire fast and they fire slow. A position opens up, and the human resources department scrambles to fill the position as quickly as possible. They hire somebody, don't check the résumé thoroughly, rush through the job interview, and lo and behold, what do they discover? The person they hired is not a good fit for the job. Then to add insult in injury, they take way too long to let the person go.

Many women make this exact same mistake in relationships. Again, they don't realize that the management of new hires—or potential partners—rests entirely in their hands. What's the answer to this dilemma? What does an effective boss learn to do?

Hire slow; fire fast.

A successful manager takes her time finding the right person for the position. Now, if someone you hired seems to be working out great, then keep that person on board. But if he's not working out, it's time to cut your losses for the sake of the business, or the relationship in this case. A manager who waits too long to make this decision inevitably becomes a frustrated manager.

One of our teachers at The Kabbalah Centre was giving a relationship lecture in Long Island a few years ago. There was a woman, who was probably 85 years old or so, attending the lecture. At the end of the lecture, she approached the teacher and said, "I really loved your talk, but I just want to tell you I've been married for 50 years." The teacher was about to congratulate her when the woman added, "They've been 50 miserable years."

The teacher assured the woman that there was still hope for the relationship, still time to turn things around. That's why the wisdom of Kabbalah needs to be shared—so that men and women can turn their relationships into sources of joy, instead of sources of misery.

DIVINE MAGNETISM

If the man is a pipeline or a channel, what is the woman? What is the structure of *her* soul? She is the Vessel. More specifically, a women's soul is like a bowl—a magnetic bowl that draws Light and provides it with form. She is a revealer of Light. She takes the energy that a man channels—all of his Divine potential—and gives it shape. She is like the glass that gives shape to the water it contains. It's like the sea and shore: The sea would just keep on flowing, were it not for the land that gives it form and structure.

Think of the female soul as a power generator or pump that draws God's energy through the channel. This power generator comes complete with an on/off switch. In other words, the woman decides when Light will be brought forth from the man's channel and into her life. She says to the man, "Yes, I want to experience your Light," or "No, I don't need your Light." She directs the flow of the energy. And that's what makes her the manager: She gives consent. She gives permission. This is the tremendous power of the Vessel.

From a strictly 1 Percent perspective, think of a man who wants to have sex with his partner. When a man makes his move, who ultimately decides whether these two people will have sex? The woman. It's the man's job to offer to share his Light until he receives clear direction from the woman on whether or not to proceed. And a man craves that direction. But it's the woman's job to know how to manage it. Think of the Light as energy that exists between two people in a relationship, with this energy being fed through a pipe from Heaven. The pipe belongs to the man, but the woman controls the valve.

You control the oxygen valve to the relationship.

This is the control that women have in relationships. As you are beginning to see, it's truly an awesome responsibility.

In the ancient kabbalistic writings, there is a saying: *A woman builds or a woman destroys.* This is followed by the question we raised at the beginning of this book: *If a good woman marries an evil man and an evil woman marries a good man, how do the relationships work out?* In both scenarios, the outcome is determined exclusively by the woman. Why? Because it's the woman's consciousness that directs the Light in both instances. So if a selfish woman thinks only of how God's energy can benefit her, her selfishness—

her ego—will prevail. It doesn't matter that the man might have the potential to transform this world and to make it a better place. If the woman's Vessel is limited or lacks structural integrity, the man's Light is wasted.

This is because the quality of the Light depends on the quality of the Vessel. If you were to pour pristine water into a dusty or grimy or cracked glass, the water would become dirty or be wasted. In the same way, if you were to channel pure Light into a corrupted or broken Vessel, that Light would never reach its full potential.

On the other hand, what happens when a woman has a large desire—a Vessel that is primed and ready to receive and manage a great revelation of Light? This woman craves more than just a nice home. She craves spiritual growth and transformation. She wants the best that the Universe has to offer in every area of her life. But if she draws men into her life with a limited ability to channel Light, she is left feeling empty, alone and disappointed by what she believes life has to offer.

Fortunately, the solution is surprisingly simple, but it requires that you do your due diligence at the beginning of your search, just like the manager who hires slow and fires fast. You must invite men into your life who have a large capacity to channel Light. I call this the Orbiting Planet scenario.

THE ORBITING PLANET SCENARIO

Imagine a solar system in which a sun is orbited by two planets. For these two planets to orbit that sun successfully, what would have to happen? First of all, they would have to be traveling in the same direction; otherwise, they would risk frequent collision. Imagine now that these two planets are people: They should want the same things out of life; in other words, they should have complementary values and similar goals. This requirement should not be confused with the passion or chemistry that you might feel at the beginning of a relationship. That's just 1 Percent information. If two planets are meant to orbit successfully, all of the logistics of long-term travel need to be taken into account—not just a tiny fraction.

What's the second requirement for these two planets? These two planets—these two people—have to be at the same altitude. That is to say, both people have to be on the same spiritual level. Their appetite for life needs to be in alignment. The size of their Vessels, their desire, has to match. If one planet is orbiting high above the other, they'll never be close enough to communicate effectively. No matter how hard they try, they'll never be on the same wavelength.

What does this mean for you? If you have a big desire for Light, don't settle for a guy who just wants to come home at the end of the day, read the paper, have dinner, and go to sleep—and do this every day for the next 50 years. Now, I'm not judging the person in this example because that's the structure of his soul. But if you long for more, have no doubt that you *will* become frustrated in a relationship with this person.

If you don't want to marry a police officer because of the stress that lifestyle entails, then don't date a police officer. I know women who have met men, and after six months or so, they decide that they don't like the man's profession so they try to change it. Don't waste your time. It's up to the man to decide how he will channel Light into this world, and it's up to the woman to decide whether the way he brings Light into this physical reality is in alignment with her goals, her values, and the direction she has chosen for her life.

There is one more requirement for these two planets. We've talked about direction and altitude. Can you guess the third condition? The third condition is speed. If one person is zooming ahead and the other person is lagging behind, this is bound to cause chaos in the future. The pace of these two entities must be the same or they risk colliding. Perhaps you've been in a relationship in which you always felt that you had to pull the other person along to get him to keep up with you. It's exhausting and ineffective. Why? Because coercion is not a pathway to experiencing Light.

Let's think about coercion for a moment. For some reason, even when their intentions are good, some people feel a need to coerce others. But does the Light or the Creator coerce us? Is God forcing us to believe in His existence? Not at all. On the contrary, we have been given the gift of free will so we can earn the discovery of *all truths*, not just the truth of God's existence. If God respects our free will and honors our opportunity to say *no*, we need to emulate that consciousness of God and not coerce others. Most importantly, a woman should never ever allow a man (or anyone else) to coerce her. If you do, you are denying the greatest gift God gave you.

So for our pair of planets to align happily, they must have the same direction, altitude, and speed, and they must be free of all coercion. Every once in a while these conditions might tip slightly off balance. One of the two parties might move a little faster, get off course for a moment, or orbit at a slightly lower altitude for a time. But as long as these anomalous states are temporary, you can work around them. Better yet, they can be opportunities for growth, and the journey can still be successful.

THE CHANNEL AND THE VESSEL IN PRACTICE

Just because your direction, altitude, and speed are in sync with that of your partner doesn't mean that you won't have some work to do. Meeting the right man is only the beginning. Without proper communication, even well-matched individuals are susceptible to the forces of entropy.

One challenge I often see when talking with women about relationships is that they sometimes communicate with men as if they were communicating with their girlfriends. But the language of men is vastly different from the language of women. And if you are unaware of this, it's easy to unwittingly say things to a man that in the world of women would be perfectly acceptable but with a man won't work at all.

I'll give you an example. Remember that a man's primary desire is to earn your love. He wants to please you. With this in mind, it's ineffective to *tell* a man to do something. But it's entirely effective to *ask* him to do something *for you*. Do you see the difference? For example, when you say, "Honey, take out the garbage," he's thinking, "Why is she always ordering me around?" But when you say, "Honey, when you get a minute, could you take out the garbage for me?" you're triggering a completely different feeling—and result. Why? Because you just gave him a chance to please you, to act according to his natural impulse.

Now I know what you're thinking. Is that really all it would take for me to get my husband to take out the trash? Can't guys see through this? Yes, we men fall for it every time. We *enjoy* falling for it. And if you don't believe me, try it out on your husband and see for yourself.

In fact, Kabbalah encourages us to put these—and all—spiritual practices to the test in our own lives before believing in their effectiveness. And yes, learning how to ask a man to take out the trash becomes a spiritual practice when your intent is to cultivate a fulfilling relationship—spiritually, emotionally, and physically. This is one practical component of the spiritual rules that govern relationships!

One final thought as it relates to men as channels of God's Light and to women as Vessels: The channel never changes; only the Vessel has the ability to change. A woman cannot change the nature of a man, but she *can* change the shape and availability of her Vessel. If a man is not bringing enough Light into a relationship, a woman does not have to keep her Vessel open in vain. It's her responsibility to seek out a channel of Light equivalent in size to her Vessel—*if and when* she so chooses. In fact, as you'll learn in the next chapter, women have the ability (and duty) to create their own Light. Spiritually speaking, a woman does not need a man. She is both the Light and the Vessel!

Rule Number Two:

A man cannot be the source of a woman's happiness.

For those of you waiting to meet the right guy and thinking that you will be happy once you do, I have a surprise for you. It's not a man's job to make a woman happy. Nor is it a woman's job to make a man happy. That's not the role of either the man or the woman. The role of men and women is quite specific, and neither job description entails "being responsible for the happiness of another." That's just not the way the Universe operates.

So what is the source of a woman's happiness? Chocolate? Sex? Silence? Good conversation? New shoes? All kidding aside, you know the answer:

It's the Light, of course.

The Light is the ultimate Cause of everyone's happiness. A man can't make you happy. He can't change the way you feel about yourself. He can't make you feel loved. He can't make you feel secure. The only thing that can make you feel these things is the Light. If you are trying to get a man to make you feel whole, then you are fighting a losing battle, and I'm guessing that there is a great deal of suffering in your relationship.

No one has to suffer, especially not a woman, because women are unique from men in another very fundamental way. According to the *Zohar*, the 2000-year-old text that contains a wellspring of kabbalistic wisdom, a woman's soul contains the attributes of both the Light and the Vessel. How is this possible? It's simple: The Light created the Vessel out of itself—therefore the Vessel contains both sharing and receiving attributes.

This distinction has far-reaching implications for women. It means a woman doesn't need a man at all. From a spiritual standpoint, she can reveal Light without any effort on a man's part. These attributes make a woman a complete system, with all the circuitry it needs. Think about it. We've all heard of woman's intuition. It works because women have the source of all answers, of all wisdom inside of them at all times—if and when they choose to tap into it.

The truth is that a man needs you much more than you need a man. Regardless of whether this is how you feel about the men in your life, it's the reality of the situation. A man needs your Vessel to manifest his potential, to manifest his Light. A woman is the Vessel for all that a man has to offer this physical world. Without it, he is just a pipeline, neither the source of Light nor the container. He's merely a middleman.

The challenge of this arrangement lies in the fact that women often fail to see their inherent Light. In fact, it seems that no matter how gorgeous a woman is or how many degrees she has, chances are that she struggles with self-esteem. Why do so many women fail to see their inherent worth? It's because spiritually, the Vessel fears that it will remain without Light or that it will never get enough.

This is the root of the Vessel's fear. This sense of impending scarcity underlies the Vessel's entire existence. And what's the irony in that? *An insufficient amount of Light within a woman's Vessel is impossible!* Infinite Light is the very core of a woman's soul; it's been there since the beginning of time. You just didn't know it until now.

Finding a good man and building a relationship upon joy and fulfillment starts with recognizing the powerful Light that exists in you—that exists in every woman. The only reason that a woman would ever doubt her worth as a human being is because she is having difficulty seeing the Lightforce that's inside of her.

Once you recognize and connect to your Light, you also recognize the need to protect and conserve it and maintain the connection. The best way to do this is by not giving away your Light too quickly. My experience is that many women tend to give themselves away before assessing the situation completely.

Remember the hiring process that we discussed before? All too often, women bring someone into their life; give themselves away to that person, and *then* start gathering information. The sequence of events is all wrong, which makes for a very ineffective hiring practice. And we all want to learn to make effective choices, especially when it comes to choosing a partner.

Before the "interview" process can even begin, a woman must recognize her potential to generate her own Light. A woman who fails to see her own Light and soul could meet dozens of qualified candidates, but not one of them would ever bring her joy. She might reap some temporary pleasure by being with these men, but she would be left feeling as empty as before. Guaranteed.

If you are already in a committed relationship, it might seem as if the interview stage of your relationship took place a long time ago. But discovering more about your partner should be an ongoing process. Once you are hired at a corporation, do the managers let you do whatever you want? Of course not. Every few months, a manager reviews your progress, right? As the CEO of your relationship, it's up to you to do the same.

If you are the type of person who needs to be with other people most of the time, if you are someone who goes out often and dreads being by yourself, you are most likely trying to find energy from someplace other than from within yourself. This way of living will get you nowhere because you're looking for Light in all the wrong places. According to the Law of Attraction, you must become *like* the Light to draw close to it. If you look outside yourself for happiness, you are relinquishing control to an external influence. You are becoming the Effect instead of the Cause. This creates disconnection, separation, and space between you and the Divine Light within. Darkness fills this space, and that is the root of all unhappiness.

So how do you connect to the Light within? You start by honoring your own interests and your passions. You start by engaging in activities that you really enjoy, not things that someone else would like you to do. You're not doing this for selfish reasons, but to connect to your soul's purpose. You don't do your friends, or your partner, or even your parents any favors if you make your life all about them.

For example, if your partner or someone you're seeing likes to watch football every Sunday at the local pub but you hate it, stop tagging along. If an activity is of little interest to you, you are not required by any law—spiritual or otherwise—to waste your energy on it. You are instantly more attractive to yourself and to everyone else when you know what you are made of—100% Light—and when you are in tune with your own nature.

We've all heard the phrase "independently wealthy." How can you become independently wealthy? You achieve this status when your assets generate enough income to allow you to live comfortably without relying on an outside job. We all need to strive to be independently wealthy when it comes to the Light. What does this mean exactly? It means that you are able to enjoy life to the fullest without relying on any outside influx of energy, whether in the form of a man, a job title, the right clothes, or anything else.

Being fully dependent on God's energy to bring you inner fulfillment means being independently happy. The Light becomes your one and only necessary asset—your cash cow, so to speak. And when you are connected to the Light inside, the Universe will supply you with an endless stream of fulfilling experiences, reflecting your inner state of being.

One of the most important ways to connect to the Light within is to stop worrying and get busy with the people around you. In other words, share! Acts of sharing, especially when they take you outside your comfort zone, are the most powerful way to connect to the deepest level of your being and to the unending sea of Light. It's a paradox. The more you worry about other people's happiness, the more the Light concerns itself with *your* happiness. The Light mirrors our actions. Remember, *like attracts like*. If you share with others and become their Light, the Light shares with you in equal measure. It is the Adversary that makes true sharing uncomfortable because it does not want you to connect to the Light. So one clue that you are truly sharing is when every bone in your body is telling you *not* to share.

So when will you meet the right guy? When you couldn't care less whether you meet the right guy or not. When you are satisfied with who you are as a person, with your connection to life, with your spiritual journey. When you are focused on helping someone else in need. When you are not *reacting* to the situation. When you're operating in this space, meeting the right guy just becomes icing on the cake. That's the secret. The more you allow fear or expectation (which is just another form of receiving) to drive you, the further you will push potential or current partners away. Fear, by its nature, does not attract effective outcomes. A strong connection to the Light, on the other hand, inevitably draws the right people near.

Your Light is like a beacon to which men are drawn. Why? Because the Light that is being channeled through a man from the Creator has one goal in mind: to find its way to you. It's the Law of Attraction in its most elemental form. Light attracts Light. Men want to earn your Light—the Light you don't even recognize inside yourself at times. Men want to work for your Light, otherwise they wouldn't really appreciate it. They don't know this logically. They don't understand it. They will never get it on an intellectual level. But their souls get it. Completely.

This is why at the soul level men are not attracted to a scantily dressed woman who walks into a room, leaving little to the imagination. To a man, a woman who presents herself in this manner offers him little opportunity to earn her affection, to earn her Light. We'll talk more in the next chapter about the importance of this point in forging long-term relationships. A man craves a woman who has made the Light her source of fulfillment. A man craves someone who is driven by love, not fear and desperation. When you know deep down inside that you don't need a man, that's the ultimate attraction.

THE RULE BREAKER

I probably shouldn't tell you this, but there's a woman here at The Kabbalah Centre who broke every rule that I am sharing with you in this book. She pursued her man from the very beginning. She was persistent. She showed all of her cards, and she still ended up with a wonderful guy and a great relationship. Do you know why? Because she didn't care about the results. Because at the end of the day, if the relationship hadn't worked out, she would have been perfectly fine. It wouldn't have crushed her. It wouldn't have changed her. Her connection to the Light would have been unaffected.

I'm talking about a woman who knows where happiness lies. I'm talking about a woman who understands that a man is not the source of her self-worth, her happiness, or her strength.

In 99 percent of the cases, most women could not pull off what she did. That's why we have the Spiritual Rules of Engagement.

AN EXERCISE: WHAT MAKES YOU HAPPY?

Take a moment and consider the activities that you really love. Do you enjoy dancing, golf, arts and crafts, cooking, or tennis? What brings you joy? Reading, walking your dog, or volunteering? Jot down whatever comes to mind. When was the last time you enjoyed this activity? What are some things you could do for yourself to make you feel wonderful about who you are?

Whatever you enjoy doing, do it this week. No, that's not soon enough. Do it today, and don't stop doing it. This is your way of revealing Light.

Rule Number Three:

The woman must defend her Light and never give it away freely.

Y ou don't have to be dressed in revealing clothes and flirting with every man in sight to be giving your Light away too easily. You could be giving it away without even knowing it. In this chapter, we'll look at some ways in which women can protect their Divine asset and set themselves up for success in a lasting, loving relationships. We'll look at which actions women take that invite committed relationships, and which ones don't.

When a woman defends her Light, she makes a man work for the honor of being with her. She presents the man with a challenge, a chance to earn her love. By doing this, she cultivates appreciation on the part of the man. He appreciates her because he has to work hard for her Light. Without appreciation, there is no Vessel for a long-term committed relationship.

SHORT-TERM VERSUS LONG-TERM

My guess is that if you're reading this book, you're interested in a long-term committed relationship rather than short-term recreational ones. What's the difference? As you might have guessed, short-term recreational relationships are the flings, the affairs, the one-night stands, the six-month relationships, even the two, three, or five-year relationships that go on longer than they should.

If you are interested only in relationships like these, if you're only interested in having fun, you're in luck—there are no rules! You can simply walk into those short-term recreational relationships at your own peril, with absolutely nothing to protect you or the Light that you possess. But a long-term, committed relationship comes complete with a set of spiritual rules that you are in the process of learning right now. These rules are designed to protect you and your Light from being intentionally or unintentionally misused.

I've heard many women say, "He was such a jerk. He took advantage of me." Yes, there are jerks out there. But there are good guys out there, too, and there are all the variations in between. If you don't effectively manage the energy exchange between you and these men, you will inevitably feel mistreated. My goal is to help you create the consciousness within yourself that will encourage the right man while discouraging men who just want to drain your energy.

The minute you decide to take responsibility for the men and relationships you bring into your life is the minute you will cease feeling used. As you'll see in this chapter, the actions that you can take to protect your Light are spiritually grounded yet incredibly practical. Let's look at some examples.

THE LOGISTICS OF THE FIRST DATE

What's a good setting for a successful first date? Many women will say dinner. But dinnertime has a built-in quality of intimacy. We often forget this, but it's true. Dinner, of course, takes place in the evening, which leads a man's mind to wonder how and where the evening will end up.

But you have more control over this than you think. How? Make sure that your first date takes place during the day. The activity you choose should be something light and casual, which provides you with an opportunity to decide whether dinner with this person is something you want. Again, this is your way of protecting your Vessel and preserving your Light.

Let's say that a man asks you if you would like to have lunch together. He says, "Can we have lunch, maybe tomorrow at 12:30?" This is a pretty straightforward situation, one that you've probably faced. But let's take it one step further. Let's say it's not just any random guy, but someone that you are interested in, which makes it all the more important to remember that this is your first opportunity to direct his energy. There may be plenty more, but this first one sets the stage.

What do you do? You express interest, but you change the time. I know you're thinking, "Do I really have to play games like this?" No, because this isn't a game. This isn't about manipulation. It's about effective management. By allowing the man to set the day and time for your date, you forfeit your status as manager. Once forfeited, this position is difficult to recover. So instead, you can respond with, "I'd love to have lunch, but tomorrow doesn't work for me, how about Thursday at 1:00?" In this way, you've given him a glimpse of your Light—you've shown interest—and he understands that he'll have to earn the rest. He sees that you already have a self-sufficient, fulfilling life without him, and he'll have to work hard to become a part of it.

Some women might say, "But what if it hurts his feelings or discourages him that I don't want to see him right away?" But don't forget: Your job is not to protect his ego; it's to protect *your* Light. Let him earn you. Let him seek you out. If he is genuinely interested, he will—and on *your* time schedule. If he's not willing to accommodate you, you've learned a critical piece of information about him from just one phone call!

PACE AND PLACE

The pace is yours to determine, as is the place. Yes, you suggest the place. Why? Because you're running the show and because this sends him a two-fold message: that you value yourself and you expect him to value you and your choices as well. What if he tells you he would like to take you to a nice place as a surprise? It's sounds tempting, but a surprise location is not first-date material. Remember this is your company, your business. Would you allow a job candidate who is scheduled for an interview suggest the location of your meeting? No, of course not. A potential employee plays by the company's rules. The company decides where the interview will take place.

REVEAL ONE HAND

An experienced interviewer lets the candidate do most of the talking during an interview. In much the same way, you'll be letting the man do most of the talking on your first date. Even if he wants to talk about you, it's your job to steer his energy away from you. You can encourage him by simply saying, "Let's talk some more about you. I'm more interested in what you have going on in your life." What man could resist hearing that?

Inviting him to talk serves multiple purposes. It encourages him to do what he is designed to do: share his Light. At the same time, it allows you to keep your Light concealed, revealing only small amounts at your discretion when you feel the time and place are right.

At the same time, by focusing your attention on him during the first date, you are creating desire in him to want to learn more about you. Most importantly, keeping your Light close at hand creates Resistance, which we'll discuss in greater detail in a moment. Resistance is the key both to creating Light between two individuals and to making the Light last forever.

TO PAY OR NOT TO PAY

As your time together draws to a close, the question of who pays for the date arises. But there really is no question here. It's your job to allow the man to pay—this is another way he shares his Light with you. If you make more money than he does, he still pays—even if all he can afford right now is a couple of slices of pizza. What about after you've been together for years? It doesn't matter. He still pays because it makes him feel as if he's taking care of you.

I often hear women say, "But won't he become resentful that I never offer to pay?" Nonsense. Let him think: *Who does she think she is?* Because his next thought will be: *I guess she thinks she's someone special. And come to think of it, that's the kind of woman I want to be with.* That's how most men think. As I said before, men are drawn to women who recognize their own Light, their own worth, their own uniqueness.

Just as it's his responsibility to pay for your coffee or lunch, it's your job to end the date first. You can plant the seed for this ahead of time by mentioning that you have another obligation after your meeting with him. It's not his business to know what your previously scheduled commitment is; even if you have nothing planned, you always have an obligation to honor your Light. And keep in mind that your first date shouldn't be long; it's designed to help you decide if this person is someone who even deserves your attention in the first place. So it's necessary to keep your time together short and with a clear end point in sight.

Why is this so important? Because the mindset that are bringing to this meeting is that you are a fulfilled, unique person with a joyful, busy life, and if things work out with him, then great, and if they don't, there are thousands of other fish in the sea. This is the energy that a man wants to feel. He may not realize this consciously, but on a soul level, he is attracted to a woman with this type of consciousness. You can see now why keeping your first outing short and sweet is to your advantage.

I WANNA GET PHYSICAL

You followed all the Spiritual Rules of Engagement and had a nice first date. You're interested. He's dropping you off when he moves in to give you a little peck on the cheek. But it doesn't stop there. You feel his hand on your side sliding up to touch you in a way that you don't think is appropriate quite yet. Just because he's making his move, does this mean he's the wrong guy? No, not at all. It just means that it's time for you to redirect his energy. But how do you handle it? After all, this can be a pretty awkward situation.

But it doesn't have to be—just move his hand. You don't have to say anything. In fact, it's far better if you don't. As we'll learn later, men communicate with actions (remember, they are sharers, doers, and proactive by nature), so if you want a man to understand you, you have to speak his language. You don't have to say, "Not yet, Honey." Just move his hand. In one motion, you've honored your Light, and effectively redirected *his*.

PRACTICING RESISTANCE

What if you are at a party and you notice the man of your dreams across the room? Don't even look at him! That's right. Spiritually speaking, your best chance of meeting the right guy and establishing the foundation for a long-term commitment starts by not even looking in his direction. Kabbalah has a name for this notion. It's called *Resistance*.

When you resist your reactive tendencies—the urge to make eye contact, the desire to flirt, the inclination to go to him before he has made his move towards you—you open yourself up to receive more Light later. If you were to act on every thought that passes through your mind, the poor man across the room would be sprinting for the door. You'd be giving your Light away all at once, and it would be blinding!

Let him talk first. Let him look at you first. Let him find you. Let him seek you out. Remember that it is the Adversary making you impatient. Each time you listen to that rash voice, you distance yourself from the infinite ocean of Light within you.

If you want to learn the specifics of practicing Resistance, I recommend the book *The Power of Kabbalah*, in which I describe the Proactive Formula. The Proactive Formula describes how we reveal Light, which involves learning to shut down our reactive tendencies, moving out of our comfort zone and old habits, and performing acts of sharing. This brings us closer to the Light. These steps, when practiced regularly, take you to a higher level of thinking and being. These steps allow you to connect to the Light within so that your external world will mirror this increased illumination that has taken place inside of you.

Now back to that party where you just spotted the man of your dreams. If you are a Type A personality—if you are typically flirtatious, assertive, and aggressive—it's time to rethink your approach. Men often interpret a flirty and aggressive woman as someone who might be fun in the short term but isn't for the long term. Often, it's merely your ego talking to his ego, with both souls being left out of the equation.

In the same way, it doesn't work to initiate a call to someone you just met or to spend a great deal of time on the phone with someone you are just getting to know. Kabbalistically, when you spend two hours talking on the phone with someone you are interested in, you're not practicing Resistance. You are not managing your energy out of care and consideration for the guy you are talking to—or for yourself. You're holding nothing back, which puts this budding relationship at an inherent disadvantage.

How? Because you're unintentionally giving the man little reason to fight for your time, your respect, and most importantly, your Light. On the other hand, when you choose to limit your time with him to 20 minutes on the phone, you're helping him to direct his energy. You are creating desire on his part—a desire to earn your love. That is an act of sharing, and it draws you closer to the Light.

Let's turn the tables for a second. Picture this: You are talking to someone on the phone whom you met recently. This man is telling you all about his past marriage and his bitter divorce. Then he launches into a blow-by-blow description of all his relationships since that time and how terrible they were. Are you turned on? No, you're probably quite turned off. You're probably thinking that this guy is pretty needy, and you'd be right. His desperation leaves you with very little to be curious about. There's no mystery, nor is there any desire left on your part to bring your Light closer to his. In much the same way, women squelch a man's desire when they reveal their entire hand all at once.

Resistance in the context of getting to know someone new means asking yourself:

Is this conversation lasting too long? What will the result be?

Is this helping the relationship or hurting it? What will the consequences be?

Am I investing too much of my Light into this relationship too soon?

Will this help my company grow or will it hurt my company?

By assessing the situation in this way, you are better able to make effective executive decisions along the way.

As I said before, if you are looking for a long-term committed relationship, there are certain rules that must be respected. If you are interested in only short-term recreational relationships, on the other hand, there are no rules. You like him; you let it happen. Resistance never even enters the picture in most short-term relationships. If you want a short-term thrill, enjoy the ride—but be willing to accept the consequences.

And there will be consequences. Any time we don't practice Resistance, either physically or emotionally, we experience a burst of short-term pleasure, but we forego our chances for long-term fulfillment. This situation is by no means exclusive to women. But women have to be particularly diligent at protecting their Light and practicing Resistance or they are susceptible to feeling used, abused, and empty after the ride is over. You can tell yourself that you were just having fun, but that excuse doesn't do your soul any good when your hope for a lasting relationship just walked out the door.

Resistance isn't something we practice for the sake of martyrdom or self-denial. Not at all. Resistance is required to activate the Light of the Creator within each of us. When women practice Resistance in the context of a relationship—when women protect the Light they have and refuse to give it away freely—they give themselves permission to enjoy a relationship built upon spiritual principles and not base-level desires and temporary indulgences. Resistance is the essential ingredient for this transformation. And these are relationships built to last.

FOR THOSE WHO ARE IN A COMMITTED RELATIONSHIP

I've talked a great deal about first dates and new beginnings. Some of you are probably wondering: *Do these spiritual rules also apply to the women who are already in a long-term committed relationship?* Absolutely. In fact, women who are already in a relationship must work equally hard at maintaining their proactive Light-consciousness as well as adhering to these spiritual principles. The moment you become complacent or reactive, a man quickly forgets that he still needs to earn your Light. If you stop protecting your most desirable asset, a man loses his desire for it. He knows that he can experience it any time he wants. The challenge is gone.

But it doesn't have to be that way. You and your partner may have been together for a long time, but the functions of the male soul and the female soul have not changed. The man's function is to share, and the women's function is to be a Vessel to receive that sharing. A man desires to please, while a woman desires to be pleased, appreciated, and respected. Through your consciousness and your actions, your partner should never forget that your love must always be earned, your Vessel should always be cared for, and your Light is a Divine treasure. In other words, you still let him pay for your dinner, he still takes out the trash for you, and you still manage his Light, even after you've been together for 50 years!

Rule Number Four:

Never believe what a man says.

I didn't want to use this rule to start off because I was worried it might give you the wrong impression. But now that you are starting to understand the rules and the spiritual context from which they arise, I think you're ready for this one. In terms of importance, this rule should be right at the top of the list: *Don't believe what a man says; just watch what he does.*

The Adversary controls our thoughts and words 99 percent of the time. The only time our soul is talking is when we resist the Adversary. Therefore, most of the words that come out of our mouths are motivated by self-interest and not soulful Light. This is particularly true of men, especially when they are in courtship mode.

For instance, the man in your life says, "Honey, I love you. Baby, I miss you. You're amazing." But he never calls, and he's rarely around. What do you believe: his words or his actions? Or maybe the guy you're currently seeing is quiet. You assume he's not interested, but rather than basing your conclusion on what he says or doesn't say, watch what he does instead. If he's quiet but sends you emails on a regular basis, gives you little gifts, or consistently chooses to spend time with you, he likes you. He may not be a talker, but his actions speak louder than words.

Why shouldn't you believe what a man says? Because in the male world, talk has far less meaning than it does for women. This is confusing for many women because in the female world, talking is an important way to exchange energy, a way to connect. But in the male world, it's not. Talking is how men build themselves up, how they get ahead, or how they calm somebody down. For most men, talking is a tool to achieve an end; it is not usually connected to truth—or to Light. Of course, there are exceptions to this, but generally speaking, men place far less value on verbal statements than women do.

HE'S NEVER AROUND

If a man you have been with for a year has been telling you that he plans on leaving his wife any day now but he still hasn't made his move, his actions are revealing the whole story. And my guess is that it's a story that your soul has known all along.

If a man chooses not to be around you, there is a good reason. He might tell you that he is a pilot or a busy doctor on call, and his story might even be true. But if a man *wants* to make time for you, he will. Why? Because he knows no other way than sharing his Light. He doesn't know how to put on brakes or close the valve—that's not a skill his soul possesses. So if he is not sharing his Light with you, he's sharing it with the world in some other way.

This is because sharing his Light is the only thing that makes a man truly happy; sharing is his nature. When he's discovered his unique way of bringing energy into this world, he feels fulfilled. Whether it's through his career or another avenue, his sole function is to bring Light to other people. When he feels as though he is achieving this goal, he'll stay in this place of sharing indefinitely—until his Light is directed elsewhere.

What do you do if you are in a long-term committed relationship and your partner is not spending enough time with you? He's taking you for granted. He's not giving you the energy that you think you deserve. What do you do? Do you sit down and have a talk with him? No. As we now know, talking does not have the same meaning for men as it does for women. Most men understand actions far better than verbal cues.

So instead of sitting down with him and attempting to have a "state of the union" address, do something fabulous for yourself that does not involve him. Go out with your girlfriends. Go have an amazing massage. Spend a day at the spa. Go hiking. Go bowling, if that's what you enjoy. Do something that reinvigorates your soul. Go share your gifts with others. Do anything that reminds you that it's not about him—it's about your relationship with the Light.

And while you're out honoring your relationship with the Light, you're not there for him. You've made yourself intentionally unavailable. And men want what they can't have. Don't forget, what's the one thing they should never have? Your Light. Your Light belongs to you. You might allow a man to bask in it from time to time, but it belongs to you, and a smart woman never gives her Light away. You might be celebrating your Golden Anniversary, but he still never owns your Light. It's yours, and it's what makes you happy.

WHY MEN CHEAT

Men operate in a world of action, a world of proactivity— that is the nature of the channel. It's in a constant state of sharing energy. And a man's actions will reveal whether he is at peace or not by the manner in which he shares his Light with the world. If you find a man who has not yet discovered his place in the world, who is not happy with his path, who hasn't defined his own terms as a man, he will cheat on you. Such cheating doesn't have to be sexually. Men can make themselves emotionally unavailable in a number of ways. They do it via television, work, alcohol, the Internet, gambling, or any other number of addictions or distractions.

Why do men cheat? Because it's something that they can be successful at when they are feeling unsuccessful at most other things in their life. They want to feel instant gratification, immediate pleasure, and short-term success. At least it's something, right? It might not be true fulfillment, but at least it takes the edge off for a moment.

The ego is a powerful force, according to Kabbalah. It is the real Satan. Satan, by the way, is the English translation of the Hebrew word for Adversary. So Satan is not a demon or devil at all. He is the ego-force of reactive consciousness that tests us all day long. If we give the ego power, if we listen to it, it can lead us down roads that take us far away from the Light of the Creator.

Men give the ego control when they buy into the lie that they must have material wealth to be successful, the right job title to feel legitimate, a sports car to have power—the list goes on. But when a man has found his way of successfully channeling God's energy into this physical plane (by sharing it with his children, through his vocation, or with a hobby, for example), he doesn't need the salary, the job title, or the sports car. The immense concentration of Light that such a man is able to bring forth puts to rest the ego and all of its trappings. The need to cheat, to use addictions or distractions, to have an emotional or physical affair doesn't enter the picture. This is simple to describe, of course, but it is not an easy place for a man to get to. It takes a lot of work and lot of tools. Fortunately, we can harness the technology of Kabbalah to that end.

The key for a woman is to find a man who is channeling Light and enjoying it, someone who doesn't need cheap external energy to keep himself motivated, someone who is driven by a lasting, internal force—or at least is on the path to discovering his unique way of sharing his gift with others. If you cannot find a man already in this state of consciousness, find one who shows promise. Then you can introduce him to this book and to these teachings. It will either resonate with him or it won't. If it does, you're on your way.

DON'T TRY TO FIGURE A MAN OUT

Many women believe that if they can assess a man's words and actions, they might be able to figure out his intentions. But it does little good to try to figure a man out. Imagine you have an employee who has been acting flaky lately by coming in late to work, turning in projects behind schedule and not returning client phone calls. You've discussed the problem with him and he's promised to make some adjustments, but his behavior isn't changing. Your business is starting to suffer. Now what do you do?

Do you spend a great deal of time wondering what thoughts are behind his erratic behavior or do you make an executive decision? An effective manager must make a business-minded decision or she risks the well-being of her entire company. Men are not designed to be figured out, which means that all a woman can do is take action. If a man is ineffective in his role at your company, then it's time for you to show him the door.

After meeting a man and anticipating his phone call, many women find themselves wondering after a few days: *How come he's not calling?* Maybe he became incapacitated in

Tibet while he was trying to climb Mount Everest. We don't know. And the truth of the situation is this:

It doesn't matter!

Your Light and your time are too precious to waste on trying to figure out the Byzantine machinations of the male mind. In fact, it's my experience that there's not nearly as much going on in a man's mind as women often think there is. If he's not calling, then it's time to let it go. That is the only action you need to take. It's that simple.

Some of you might not be content with this approach. You'll decide it would be best to go and save him in Tibet; at least that way you can see first-hand that his cell phone wasn't working and that's why he hasn't called you. You'll figure out what expedition he is on and you'll climb to his aid on some treacherous mountainside. But despite the fact that you prevented him from freezing to death, he's not going to fall madly in love with you. In fact, he's probably feeling annoyed that you tracked him down. After all, you've intruded on his adventure! You've squelched his Light!

Making decisions based on fear and insecurity is a reactive, ineffectual way of living, and it's no way to honor or connect to the source of Light within you. What can you do instead? You can choose to resist the urge to "figure him out," and base your decisions solely on his behavior. By doing so, you become a more effective decision-maker—not to mention a woman grounded in certainty and strength.

Rule Number Five:

The woman must choose a
man that she can support.

L ove the pipe. Love the conduit. Love the way he brings energy to the world. If you can't, then don't, but don't believe for a moment that you're going to change him. Remember what I said before: You can't change the channel; you can only change the size, shape, and availability of your Vessel. So if you cannot support the manner in which he channels his energy into this world— maybe his job is too dangerous for you, or perhaps the church, mosque, or synagogue in which he is involved isn't in sync with your beliefs—then he's not the man for you. Move on.

I know this sounds harsh, but think about it. If his channel is not a good fit for your Vessel, then you will constantly feel frustrated, which jeopardizes your most important relationship—your relationship with the Light. Supporting and appreciating the way your man brings Light to the world strengthens your connection to the Creator. The opposite is also true. If you are wasting your energy trying to change the man you are with, your relationship with the Light takes a back seat. Nobody wins in this case. Life becomes one short-circuit after another.

If you can't support his livelihood, his personality, or his habits—if you are unable to support his particular brand of Light—that's okay, but please don't waste *your* precious Light trying to reconfigure his raw materials, his essence, halfway through the relationship. It will be futile. Raw materials are raw materials. It's *his* consciousness, *his* being, *his* DNA. You're not going to rewrite that.

Consider this: If you had a graphic designer on staff whose design style was cutting-edge but your company had a more sedate, conventional image, would you try to convince the designer to change his style? Or would you encourage him to find a company that fully appreciated his unique visual sensibility? You know the answer. Keeping someone in a box of your own design doesn't allow him room to grow. It only serves to smother his Light so that no one can benefit from it.

Too many women meet men and want to change them. The number one complaint I hear is: *If only he would change, our relationship would be better.* But what if he doesn't want to change? You can't force someone to change. But this doesn't make you powerless, either. You can always choose to support him or choose not to support him. Those are two powerful options.

SPINNING TOPS

Make it easy on yourself. Choose a man you can support, a man you don't wish to change, a man who channels Light in a way that you can appreciate. I have seen women choose to be with men who don't yet know what makes them happy. These men are spinning tops, wandering directionless. Sometimes all these guys need is just a little focus or direction, and the right woman can help them with that. But sometimes there's just not enough material there to work with.

It's up to the woman to recognize when a man doesn't have a defined path. How do you do this? Just watch what he does. Observe his actions and how he brings the energy of the Light into this world. All the answers are right there in front of you. Just leave your hopes out of the picture and take a good, clear look. Once he has moved through your evaluation process, then you can decide if he is someone that your company can stand behind. It's up to you to choose wisely or risk wasting the time and energy of your company.

SHOWING SUPPORT

One way to show support on a practical level is by letting your man know when he has done something that pleases you. If he has fixed a doorknob or a stuck window jamb in your apartment or house, here's your opportunity to make him feel as if he just patched a hole in the Universe. You can do that with a look, a nice dinner, a kiss, or an admiring touch. How does a man interpret these actions? He thinks: *She likes the way I bring her Light. She loves me; she trusts me; she supports me.*

A man, by his nature, likes to feel that the Light he has shared has not been in vain. Moreover, when he shares and you receive, you encourage the flow of Light and the momentum of energy between the two of you. That's why it is so important to acknowledge his effort and reinforce his ability to channel Light.

WITHDRAWING SUPPORT

My sincere hope is that this book will help you to choose the right man, a man whom you can support and one who takes care of you spiritually. But what if your man does something that you can no longer support, something that violates the Universal Laws to which you subscribe? In the last chapter, we discussed different forms of cheating, both physical and emotional. So what happens when you can no longer support the way that your designated pipeline is bringing Light?

If you cannot support him any longer, then the decision has already been made on a spiritual level. Your heart is no longer in the game.

If his energy is being spent elsewhere, he's no longer fulfilling his role in your relationship. This realization might feel terribly uncomfortable (that's fear and ego rearing their heads), but because you understand how the Universe operates, you ultimately subscribe to a Higher Law than your man. This higher authority is the Light. And the Light is what you're really after anyway. You might still love him, but as the relationship manager, you will tolerate certain things and not others. This means drawing a line in the sand and being prepared to act if it's crossed. As you know, the structure of the female soul is a Vessel—a Vessel with defined walls and inherent structure, like a fortress. And like any fortress, it must be protected.

Harlan Hendricks, a famous psychologist, said it best: *In order for a marriage to work or any long-term committed relationship to work, you have to be willing to do everything for the other person, including leaving them.* If this is the decision you must make, rest assured that you are not walking away empty. Your Vessel has been bursting at the seams with Light from the very beginning of time, and it will continue that way forever. This is your role in life.

Rule Number Six:

Attraction is based on karma.

O
ne of the teachers at The Kabbalah Centre has a sister who at one time had a tendency to date men with names that rhymed. The folks close to her called it the Harry-Barry-Larry phase. No joke: The name of every guy she dated rhymed with the previous guy's name. It was virtually the same name every time, with only the slightest variation. She finally had to ask herself, "Why do I keep drawing the same type of person into my life over and over again?"

It's a common phenomenon, and let me tell you why. According to Kabbalah, you have lived many lifetimes before this one, and your prior incarnations dictate whom you are attracted to in your current life. Why do you think you are attracted to some men and not to others? It's simple—you've met them before.

PRIOR KNOWLEDGE

According to Kabbalah, you can't be attracted to something unless you have prior knowledge of it. For instance, what if I asked you, "Do you like that new song they've been playing on the radio?" You wouldn't be able to answer that question unless you had heard the song—or tasted the food, or seen the commercial. If you haven't experienced something yet, you can't have an opinion on the matter.

It works the same way in relationships. Prior experience with something or someone creates karma, or the residue from past actions. This explains why you have a surge of emotion when you meet certain men, even though it doesn't make any rational sense. You don't know this person, right? You don't know what he's capable of or what he's not capable of, what his potential is, or what his limitations are. But somehow you've heard his "song" before.

Kabbalistically speaking, very often when you meet a man, it's because you had some type of prior relationship with that individual. The roles might have been different in a past life, but you knew one another. You might have been friends or relatives, or maybe you traveled in the same community of people. Now you might be thinking: *So I might be attracted to my son from a past life. That doesn't sound very kosher!* But remember this: Who we are in this 1 Percent Reality is just the mask we wear. Our bodies, titles, relations, and names are only of the physical world. Our true selves belong in the spiritual 99 Percent Reality where there is only One Unified Soul.

SOUL MATES REVISITED

Earlier we discussed how your soul's other half was torn from you when the Original Vessel shattered at the beginning of time. It is now your soul's job to find its other half again. Lifetime after lifetime, you build your Vessel and strengthen your connection to the Light until one day your Vessel becomes large enough, your Light bright enough, to attract your soul mate to your life. But there are others in your life who are intended to guide your soul along its journey as well. We can call these people soul mates, too, because spiritually, we are all one and the same—we are all parts of the Original Vessel.

You can have a best friend or a business associate who is your soul mate. Your brother or sister can be your soul mate. Soul mates are people with whom you have a particularly strong connection. Your paths have crossed before in another lifetime, and now these people are taking on roles in your current life to help you transform to the next level of consciousness. And you are here to do that for them as well. You are spiritual partners.

I know a lot of people who have brothers and sisters, but they don't have a soul mate relationship with them, even though they are family. They simply don't feel the connection. The connection is there, though. All of us are connected, but because of the veils that blind us, we often cannot see what we subconsciously know. But if you have a family member or a lover in your life, they are there for a very specific reason. They have appeared in this incarnation to give you the opportunity to move closer to your Divine potential. This person is here to help you correct your spiritual path, to help reveal a challenge or obstacle that you are meant to overcome in this lifetime. In Kabbalah, this is called *tikkun*, or correction.

Rav Isaac Luria wrote about the concept of soul mates. He said that for you to meet your soul mate, you have to cross an ocean. The Ari explained that by this he meant an ocean of consciousness. You have to transform yourself, to change the way you think, which involves the same degree of effort that it would take to cross a physical ocean.

Bear in mind that 500 years ago, you didn't cross an ocean by hopping on a Virgin Atlantic flight. No, crossing the ocean took weeks of travel in ships that were often unsafe and cramped, and there was no guarantee that the conditions would be any better at your destination. How many of us are prepared to go through that kind of transformation to meet our soul mate? Few people, when really honest with themselves, want to go through the effort of such deep, psychic work and pain. Most people would rather die than change to the degree that we're talking about because most people don't like change.

My own wife, Michal, underwent this degree of pain during our courtship. When it became clear to our families that Michal and I were in a serious relationship, the Rav let it be known that he did not approve of my choice of a potential wife. The reader should understand that my father is the spiritual leader of The Kabbalah Centres worldwide, and he is respected and lovingly revered by students all over the globe. The Rav is larger than life. People literally trust the Rav with their lives.

Michal, who was a dedicated student and full-time volunteer at The Kabbalah Centre, was shattered by the Rav's disapproval, for she deeply loved and respected him. Michal knew that all her friends in The Kabbalah Centre would know what had happened. She could have run for cover. She could have given up after failing to get the Rav's approval. But she didn't. She embraced the pain. She knew she had to connect to the Light within and not worry about the approval of others if she really felt a connection to me.

The pain and ego-bashing she went through paid off. Today, the Rav loves her like a daughter. My mom loves her like a daughter. Michal also transformed in the process and experienced tremendous growth. Was it worth the pain? To find this, Michal and I just look at our wonderful children, the life we now have, and most importantly, at the people all over the world whom we have been fortunate enough to support by sharing these powerful teachings. Losing one's ego is a small price to pay to help effect change in the lives of others.

From my own perspective many years later, I know the Rav took the Ari's wisdom to heart and knowingly created the "ocean" that Michal's consciousness needed to cross to allow a true soul mate connection to take place. Such is the life of a kabbalist. Such is the path of Kabbalah.

Most of us would prefer to stay in our comfort zone and avoid such pain. We don't want to give up our chaos at the expense of the Light. You might not consider your habits, fears, and insecurities chaotic, but if they prevent you from experiencing life the way life is meant to be experienced, then as far as Kabbalah is concerned, it's chaos.

The *Zohar* tells us that often a woman is ready for a deep, spiritual partnership while the man is not. He often has to marry several different women or be a serial dater until he's ready to be with his true soul mate. So if you meet a guy who has been married and divorced a few times, it's not necessarily a bad thing. If he has used those experiences as opportunities for growth—if he has learned from his mistakes—then his consciousness is evolving, and perhaps the next relationship around, he'll be ready to channel his Light into the perfect Vessel—a woman who will help him to realize his full potential.

And sometimes two soul mates are not ready at the same time for a soul mate relationship: The Light revealed would be too great, and their Vessels aren't prepared to handle the load quite yet. When this is the case, you might have to wait until your next relationship, or even your next lifetime, before your consciousness is ready to receive everything the Creator intends for you. This doesn't mean that your present moment is a waste—on the contrary! The present moment is vital to our spiritual transformation. In this moment, we must take every action we can to learn, to grow, to increase the size of our Vessels so we'll be ready when the time is right.

When two people with common goals finally come together, love each other, respect each other, and understand the Spiritual Rules of Engagement, there is nothing more powerful than that. They are both subscribing to a higher cause—the Light. That's the ultimate situation—for him and for her. At the end of the day, it's about the Light and helping support one another's connection to the Light. That is a soul mate relationship.

Rule Number Seven:

Fear of rejection is an illusion.

T he Light *always* loves you, which means that fear of rejection is based on an illusion perpetrated by the Adversary. Fear of abandonment is also based on an illusion. These are both fears cultivated by that second voice and designed to keep you from recognizing the Light inside of you.

Men, in general, don't fear rejection in the same way that a woman does. Why? Because spiritually, the Vessel (the woman) always has a fear of not being filled with Light—despite the fact that she already possesses it. This means that the spiritual work of a woman is to recognize and to cultivate a steadfast relationship with the Light inside of her, and not to look for energy outside of herself.

This doesn't mean that you have to love yourself; you just have to be willing to love the Light that's inside you. Even if you are in a place right now where you can't love yourself for whatever reason, there is something inside you that you *can* love—something that is constant and eternal. That something is the Light.

When we are unable to recognize our Light, we feel empty. It's only the illusion of emptiness, but it feels like emptiness, nonetheless. So what do we do? We crave something

to fill this perceived vacuum. And once we've found someone who we think is filling the hole inside, we worry inces-
santly that he or she will leave us and we will be left feeling
that terrible emptiness all over again. But the irony is that we
were never empty to begin with. Still, this fear can be quite
convincing and can manifest itself in a number of ways.

To illustrate the hidden influence of fear, I've included here
the following scenario written by a woman we'll call
"Frank's Girlfriend":

*I have a history of being attracted to people who aren't good for
me. The men I choose aren't abusive; they're just emotionally
unavailable. When a good potential mate comes around, I'm
attracted to him for a month or so, but then I tire of him. One
day I want to make a commitment to this guy and the next day
I'm thinking he's too much of a geek.*

*This happened last summer with Frank. We stopped seeing each
other, but I continued to run into him at friends' gatherings once
in a while. Soon I started feeling something for him again. We
started dating again, although I know he's not "the one." I'm
now 31 and I feel like I'm never going to find the love of my life.
I sometimes think that my idea of how it's supposed to work is
distorted by all the romantic movies I've seen. I was raised by a*

single mom. I haven't seen my father since I was three. Could I have abandonment issues?

The scenario that Frank's Girlfriend describes is common for many women. You meet somebody and you think you like him, but then you're not sure. "Maybe he's not the one after all," you think. When our fears of rejection begin to surface, they often manifest in a tendency to focus on the inadequacies of our potential partner, and we lose that initial feeling of attraction. But it's not about him. It's not about that one annoying habit or the way he dresses. You can work around those things. This doubt—this fear—is about you.

When a woman feels insecure in a relationship, when she fears rejection or abandonment, she often starts looking for reasons to leave first—to beat her partner to the punch in an attempt to minimize any future pain. She might begin to push him away by unwittingly emasculating him, saying things that are unsupportive or that would make him doubt that she trusts him and his ability to be a channel for her. These reactions are a defense mechanism skillfully designed to protect the woman's ego—and to keep her locked into a cycle of fear and loneliness.

Does this sound like you? Do you always seem to find fault with every man who comes into your life, when in reality, the problem might be your own fears? If so, congratulate yourself for taking the first step in recognizing this tendency within yourself. With this knowledge, you can make a conscious effort to redirect your thinking towards the good qualities that attracted you to him in the first place.

Rest assured, you will always have doubts because there is no perfect man out there, just as there is no perfect woman. But by going back to what initially attracted you to this person in the first place and by exercising greater patience as you enter this stage of the relationship, you have a far better chance of recognizing the *right* relationship when it enters your life. Most importantly, by remembering that you are full of Light and perfectly complete without a man, you begin to see that there is no reason to fear being abandoned. You couldn't be abandoned if you tried: God's Light will always be with you. It's up to you to acknowledge and accept this profound truth. It's a life-changer.

THE ISOLATOR

Perhaps your fear of rejection keeps you in total isolation. Perhaps you can't even get out the door to meet a man, let alone push one away. You've taken the principle of protecting your Light and your Vessel to the extreme, and as a result, you're miserable. You've put your faith in the negative voice of the Adversary, instead of the limitless potential and strength of the Light. If your desire is to have a man with whom you can share your Light but you are holed up at home alone every night, you're bound to feel unsatisfied.

What can you do? You can resist your reactive nature, which is to remain at home, and you can make yourself visible. In this case, going out with your friends is practicing Resistance because you are resisting your desire to remain alone and in fear. By doing so, you are opening yourself up to experience more Light in your life.

You can't sit at home all day and expect Mr. Right to find you, which means you have to put yourself in social situations. It's not about where you go. I sometimes hear people say, "You're not going to meet a guy in a bar or at a club." But you might. You might because that's where people go to meet. But wherever you go, you still have to follow the rules and let the man approach you. Among all the vultures at a bar or club who are just looking to score a one-night stand, there may be a few gems who were dragged along to keep their friends company.

But again, it's not about where you are. You could be at the library, the bus stop, the coffee shop, the bar, The Kabbalah Centre, the bookstore, the airport. You could be anywhere. Location has nothing to do with it; it's about willingness to be open to possibility and to follow the spiritual rules we have been discussing—despite any fears you might have about being rejected. Rejection is all an illusion, remember? It's an illusion that will keep you in seclusion until you decide to trust that the Light will always provide for your needs and just get out there!

AN EXERCISE: THE POSITIVES AND NEGATIVES

Before this chapter draws to a close, I would like to ask you to perform an exercise, which I hope will provide you with some revealing insights. I would like you to think about the long-term committed relationships that you have had in your life. Think about each of the men you have seriously dated, been engaged to, or married. Close your eyes and remember the first time you saw each of these men. Think of them individually and recall the first time you spoke, the first time you interacted or went out on a date, maybe even the first time you made love. Recall their personalities, the jokes they told, and the clothes they wore. What attracted you to them? Was it an instant attraction or did it grow over time?

Now visualize the first time you noticed there was a problem—the first time you felt there were issues or frustrations. How did that make you feel? What did you do? Recall how the relationship progressed and how it finally ended. Did you break it off, or did he? How did that feel? Sit with these thoughts and feelings for a moment.

When you feel that you have visualized each relationship from beginning to end, take a sheet a paper and make a column for each man. If you have seriously dated four men, you will have four columns, each with a different name at the top. Under each man's name, write down a list of one-word attributes, positive and negative, that come to mind about that man. For instance, for one man you might write *warm, generous, kind, irresponsible, procrastinating, organized, stubborn, cynical*, etc. Just let the words come out naturally.

Once you have written down a number of traits for each man, I want you to put a positive or negative sign next to each attribute, depending on whether you consider that trait to be positive or negative. For instance, some people consider being organized a positive trait, while others might find an overly organized person annoying. Decide whether each trait is positive or negative, based on your own experience. After you have done this, I would like you to circle all of the positive traits and underline all of the negative traits so that you can clearly distinguish them.

Then I'd like you to go through all the positive traits for each man and number them according to what you liked the most and what you liked the least. The item with a number "1" beside it is the trait you liked the best, the item with a number "2" is the trait you liked the second best, and so on. Then do the same for the negative traits. The item with a number "1" beside it is the trait you disliked the most, and so on.

Finally, on a separate sheet of paper, draw a big circle with a horizontal line through the middle. In the top part of the circle, I want you to write down the *positive* traits that received a number "1." Only a positive trait that received a number "1" will go in the top part of the circle. In the bottom, write down all of the *negative* traits that received a number "1" or a "2."

Now take a moment to look over what you've written. What do you notice? Does anything stand out for you? My guess is that you can draw some pretty interesting conclusions from this exercise. Here are some conclusions that women who completed this exercise during a class at The Kabbalah Centre drew for themselves.

What I noticed, which kind of scared me a little bit, is that the men that had the best qualities—by best, I mean the positive ones like caring and giving— are the men that I pushed away and that I, for whatever reason, ended those relationships. And the one that I thought was the love of my life—the one that I wanted more than anything--is the one that had the most negative qualities.

I just noticed that all of the negative qualities that I found in the guys whom I've been with are the same negative qualities that my dad has.

I think that the negative traits I saw in them were actually my own. I'm seeing my own traits that I wasn't really recognizing. The men were a mirror of my own traits.

A lot of my significant relationships were based on what other people thought of these men—like if they were successful or they were the most popular guys in high school. Their own traits had little to do with my choices. It was more about what other people thought.

I realized that it was all about me. All of the good traits were about how he treated me, how much he was interested in me and in love with me, and the negative traits were all about how he was not emotionally open with me. Every trait was relative to me. I was pretty wrapped up in myself in these relationships.

The men in my life have been very different. I've been with men who are spiritually deep. I've been with very creative men, but what I found was that they all have something in common. They're all playful, they're fun-loving, they have a great sense of humor. They are creative and artistic and intelligent. I don't see my father in these traits, nor my mother. It's almost like I'm seeking a partner who I can be joyful with and share with— someone who makes life fun.

You might have had similar insights, but every woman will discover something unique to herself in this exercise. Maybe you discovered your tendency to attract certain types of men, or your tendency to hold on too tightly, or to push off at the slightest hint of discord.

Many women find that they are attracted to men who are versions of their fathers, or alternately, to men who are the exact opposite of their fathers. Why is this? A father is the first male role model in a woman's life. It makes sense that some women would have a strong need to bring someone into their lives who can provide those things (physical or emotional) that they didn't receive from their father—or alternately, someone who doesn't have the qualities they don't like about their fathers. It's a tendency that we need to be aware of, and I see it come up often.

What happens if the negative traits you see in the men you have been with are negative traits in yourself? Or if the traits you have listed for the men in your life seem to trigger your negative qualities—pushing your buttons, so to speak. This occurs by design. It's part of your *tikkun*. Remember that *tikkun* is all about spiritual growth, and we all have lots of growing to accomplish in this lifetime. We're all in that boat, right? That's why we're here. There is no shortcut for ridding yourself of your negative traits, or your garbage as we call it in Kabbalah. Your garbage is your doubts, fears, insecurities and low self-esteem, and we all have the responsibility in this lifetime to transform our garbage into Light.

Every one of the negative qualities that you pinpointed in this exercise—regardless of whether it's in the men you have been with or in you—is a blockage that is keeping you from experiencing true fulfillment. If you wrote "stingy" as one of your partner's negative traits, ask yourself, "Why did that bother me? Why did that push my buttons? Is there an aspect of myself that I need to transform?" Yes, your partner's traits might have driven you crazy, but that is exactly what they were designed to do—in order to reveal those traits and tendencies within you that need spiritual attention.

The point of this exercise is not to leave you brooding over your past, but to help you appreciate it. The men you brought into your life, the decisions you made, and the way you negotiated each relationship are exactly as they should be. These were precisely the experiences you needed to bring you here to this moment: reading this book and learning how to transform your ways of acting and being to the next level of consciousness.

The Four Phases

Y ou're learning the rules. You're catching on. You're starting to see the Universe in a larger context, and you're beginning to see the role you play in your relationships. But where is this all going? Every relationship has phases, turning points, and guideposts to help you know where you are in the adventure. When you come to know and recognize these different phases, you gain the knowledge to apply the Spiritual Rules of Engagement with confidence. You are less likely to be surprised by plot twists and more likely to be prepared for them.

FIRST PHASE

The first stage is that rush of energy you feel when you have just met someone to whom you are strongly attracted. It's often referred to as puppy love, lust, or the honeymoon phase. You know this phase. You meet some guy, and before he even says hello, you're already imagining walking down the aisle with him, right? The energy is coming to you unfiltered, full throttle. You are experiencing lots of Light, all at once, and it feels marvelous.

The first phase is like a free gift—a present from the Universe that you do not have to earn. When you meet a guy and you get turned on intellectually or sexually, did you do anything for that? Think about it. Did you earn it? Did you perform some powerful act of Resistance? Probably not. It came easily—like grabbing a low-hanging fruit and taking a juicy bite. It was practically handed to you.

So what's the purpose of the first phase? Without a first phase, you'd never get hooked, right? It's as if you'd been blindfolded and hit over the head with a hammer. In the first phase of the relationship, you feel drunk with love.

The initial phase of a relationship is like a firecracker. It's a burst of light and noise, but if you're not used to firecrackers—if you're not careful—you can get hurt. But there is something far better than a flashy firecracker. A candle. Why? Because a candle shares slowly and steadily. A candle is like a long-term, committed relationship. Yes, there is the occasional spark, but its steady glow is what makes it so beautiful.

So it's okay to enjoy the first phase—it's a gift to you—but if you're looking for a long-term relationship, you will have to work to fan the flames and keep the Light burning in the relationship. It will never come as easily as it did during this initial phase.

The first phase can last for one date, one week, or several months. It depends on the individuals involved—their consciousness, their past experiences, even their age. Younger people tend to stay in the first phase longer because they usually enter into a relationship with less baggage. The gap between the first phase and the second phase could be ten minutes or it could be ten weeks or ten months. It's different for everyone.

SECOND PHASE

So what's the second phase? The second phase is when something happens. Think about movies or good novels for a moment. How do most stories start? They usually start off with a scene from everyday life. The farmer is tending to his farm, the bartender is at his bar, or the attorney is getting into her car and driving to work. But how long can you watch that? Not very long. You want something to happen, right? You don't want to watch corn growing or people sitting in traffic for hours at a time. No, you crave some excitement; after all, you paid good money to see this movie or read this book.

But in real life when something happens in your relationship to bring the honeymoon phase to an end, you're not so happy. You may be disappointed or frustrated by the arrival of everyday problems. Now instead of feeling frustrated, you can simply note the arrival of a new phase. You can say, "Ah, it's the second phase. I knew this was coming. Something is supposed to happen now."

So what happens exactly? Some challenge or difficulty is presented. It could happen on the first date, or it could happen in the second year of marriage. The second phase is when you first notice a problem, and the rose-colored glasses you've been wearing to this point come off. This is when the puppy love has begun to wane, and you begin to realize that in front of you is a human being who has both positive and negative attributes. In a movie or literary work, this is referred to as *rising action*. In other words, things are starting to heat up, for better or worse.

This might feel problematic, but what's really happening is that you are being presented with an opportunity to become a more powerful woman—an opportunity to grow and become a higher version of yourself. The second phase is about not running for the hills at the first sign of distress.

Again, is there a perfect man out there? No. Every man has his idiosyncrasies. You know that now. It's not about finding the perfect *man*; it's about finding a perfect *partner*.

During the second phase, something shifts. A question arises that takes you out of that first phase. That question is often: *Can I support this person in front of me?* It's not about supporting the man you *think* is in front of you or the man you hope one day will be in front of you. Look directly at the *actual* man who is standing before you and ask yourself, "Can I support this person?" He's a cop; can you support the fact that he's a cop? Or he's an obstetrician who will be away all hours of the night delivering babies, even when you need him; can you support that 100 percent? Because if you can't, that's perfectly fine. But now is the time to be honest about it.

These questions are a test of your true desire. In fact, the second phase is really the birth of true desire—not lust, but a true willingness to push beyond the challenge that has presented itself. In the first phase, the desire came easily, without any effort. But in the second phase, you have to support that desire yourself, now that the first phase energy is wearing off.

It might feel like a letdown, but the situation now is really an opportunity for growth in disguise. How? It lets you practice Resistance, which is the key to true fulfillment. If your reactive nature tells you to run at the first sign of unease, this time you're going to wait out the storm instead. If your nature is to grin and bear it and remain in an unfulfilling relationship, this time you're going to choose to walk away. Resistance means taking the higher road, not the easy way out.

If, after careful consideration, you decide that the relationship is not in your soul's best interest, it's time to move on. Or if the man you are seeing decides he is no longer interested, it's time to allow him to continue on his journey. Either way—regardless of whether it's your choice or his—don't forget to allow yourself to mourn the relationship. Give yourself the opportunity to feel every emotion that comes up. Do not hide from your pain. People who mourn losses properly are more likely to move on to healthier relationships in the long run. People who repress their emotions and try to move on to the next relationship as quickly as possible wind up hauling a lot of negative energy around—at least until they are ready to process those unhappy or bitter feelings.

If, on the other hand, you decide that you really do want this relationship, that your desire is real, then you move into the third phase. And if you thought the second phase was challenging, the third phase is the real test.

THE THIRD PHASE

The third phase challenges you to discover just how badly you really want this man and this relationship in your life. In the second phase, you began to see him as a human being. In the third phase, you see him at his worst, and he sees you at yours. Maybe he's made some mistakes or practiced poor judgment. How much love do you have for him now? Maybe you're broke because he just blew all of the money in your savings account. Perhaps he's been dishonest and you're devastated. Perhaps you've been dishonest and he's devastated. Maybe the conflict is more subtle. The third phase doesn't always look like a scene from a soap opera, but some level of opposition or frustration is at play here. Reality has set in, and you're left wondering how to move forward.

In the third phase, you ask yourself, "Am I willing to move to a higher level? Am I willing to become a better person to make this relationship all that the Creator meant it to be?" These are some pretty powerful questions, and while you struggle to figure out the answers, the journey you are on can become quite rocky. All of this turmoil, however, inevitably guides you towards a major turning point in the story of the relationship. The third phase offers you a chance to become a hero in your own movie, and here's why.

What is a hero willing to do at the climax of any good movie? She's prepared to do whatever it takes—even to die, if necessary. In fact, that is what makes a hero—the willingness to die for a higher cause. Imagine Bruce Willis risking his life to try to save the Earth in *Armageddon* or Frodo trying to save the Middle Earth from Sauron in *The Lord of the Rings*.

Needless to say, I don't mean to imply that you must be willing to physically leave this world, but you do have to make a vital decision about the person you want to become. During the third phase, you have to decide if you're willing to sacrifice your current identity for the sake of establishing a more spiritually-grounded version of yourself. We're not talking about change; we're talking about transformation—evolving your consciousness so you become more aligned with what the Creator intends for you.

So, the question becomes: *Am I more likely to become all that God intends for me to be, both within this relationship and outside of this relationship?* Either way you answer this question—if you answer it honestly—you will be sacrificing who you are in this moment. You will be letting go of your current way of thinking and moving into a more evolved consciousness—one in which your relationship with God and the Light becomes most important.

Ask yourself:

Is this relationship a reflection of the Light? If not, does it have the potential to be? If not, why am I still here?

How am I acting in this relationship? Am I needy or confident? Am I receptive or closed off? Am I the person God intends me to be?

Am I looking at this relationship spiritually? Am I being an effective manager of the Light that I am receiving? Am I being as loving and supportive as I could be?

What do I need to be doing in my life to best reveal the Light inside of me?

I meet many women—and men—who continue to make the same mistakes over and over and over again because they are struggling against so much. They're fighting against past incarnations, their childhood experiences, the influence of their parents. This is hard work. But with perseverance—and the timely help of some kabbalistic tools—you can break through. The third phase is when we break old, ineffective patterns and decide to support a higher cause, a deeper purpose.

You might decide to stay in your committed relationship and do everything in your power to make it work because it has the potential to reveal Light and goodness. Or you might decide to walk away from a chronically unhappy partnership in order to develop trust in the Light and its ability to fulfill your needs. Whether you stay or go, the third phase marks a distinct turning point in your relationship with the Light in your life, and subsequently with the man in your life. But the Light always comes first; it is the foundation upon which all deeply satisfying relationships are built.

FOURTH PHASE

The fourth phase is the resolution phase—the result of asking yourself the tough questions, making a decision, and accepting the outcome. Did you decide to be the hero in your movie or did you decide to be a victim? Did you decide to grow spiritually or did you fall back into old patterns? How did your movie end, and did you like the ending you chose? Would you prefer a different ending next time? If so, you have the power to change your actions and your outcomes. You are the director of your own movie.

If you're in a long-term, committed relationship, the four phases just keep repeating over and over and over again. Just like the director of a movie who has to film a scene repeatedly until he or she gets it just right, you and your partner might have to revisit the same issues over and over as a couple until you come to a solution you can both agree on. One moment, you might be in a heated argument, but by the end of the night, you are making love. You've just moved from one phase to the next; that's what couples do. You're going to bug each other; that's part of the deal. It's part of the correction process, and you don't get a free pass from the process just because you were lucky enough to meet your soul mate and get married. The four phases continue in a relationship, and if you remain open to what the relationship has to teach you, you will grow increasingly closer as a couple—and the Light you generate together will increase exponentially, too.

A HIGHER PURPOSE

What makes a relationship deeply fulfilling? A higher purpose. What is that higher purpose? Striving to bring more Light to the world. Does this purpose sound too abstract or ambitious? It's really not; in fact, it's profoundly practical. It starts with a very simple question: *How can I share? How can I share within my marriage or relationship, and how can I share outside of my marriage or relationship?* Think of it this way: If the focus of your relationship is merely about being together all the time, then you're not bringing much Light to the world at large.

The reason Kabbalah encourages people to share is not because it's morally or ethically the right thing. Sharing is the key to happiness; sharing is how a person becomes fulfilled. Why? Sharing is the nature of the hidden Light of the Creator. Therefore, the more we share, the more we emulate the Light. Then, according to the Law of

Attraction (*like attracts like*), we move closer to the Light and the world around us reflects this added illumination. So, in fact, we share out of greed—albeit an enlightened form of greed for the soul, not foolish greed that serves the ego.

The *Zohar* says that the highest degree of assistance that one human being can give another human being is to help that person move closer to the Light. We do this by helping one another realize our true potential. Ask yourself, "Do I have a higher purpose in my life?" If your answer is no, if you are investing all of your energy into the world of the 1 Percent (the world of physical appearance, emotion, and money) and if you continue to do this, your search for a deeply satisfying relationship will be in vain.

A fulfilling relationship with a man starts with you and your desire to discover that passion—that purpose—that moves and transforms you. Once you've begun to uncover your higher purpose, it becomes easier to find someone who is on a similar path. Your soul mate doesn't have to be somebody who is studying Kabbalah, but it has to be someone whom you respect, someone whose way of bringing Light into the world is something you can support. Your parallel spiritual paths will be the glue that binds you together. You will become those two planets I spoke of earlier—moving in the same direction, at the same speed, and at the same altitude.

MY MOM AND THE RAV

My mom, Karen, and my dad, the Rav, are an amazing example of two individuals who came together for a higher purpose—to complete a mission that was far bigger than the both of them. You would never have guessed that their relationship would reveal so much Light to the world. After all, on the surface, you couldn't imagine two more different people!

Their wedding picture says it all. There's the Rav standing in his full orthodox attire, complete with that *streimal* (the one my mom eventually tossed over the balcony), a long black coat, his prayer belt, and a long beard. My mom, on the other hand, is wearing a white mini dress, a blonde bob, and those little white pumps that were in fashion at the time. The contrast between them in the picture is almost comedic, they could not have been more different on the 1 Percent level. But on the 99 Percent, it was a totally different story. They shared a common spiritual vision, and together, they have helped spread the message of Kabbalah to millions of people. Without their *combined* efforts, the wisdom of Kabbalah would have remained hushed and inaccessible, as it had been for centuries. That is the awesome power of relationships.

Four years ago, the Rav experienced what doctors diagnosed as a stroke. It was a difficult time, and my mom had to make some important decisions regarding the type of consciousness she wanted to have moving forward. It would have been easy for her to fall into victim mode, but she didn't. She decided that her most important relationship is ultimately with the Light, and that it's her responsibility to continue serving that higher purpose, even if the Rav is not able to channel God's Light in the same way he did before. That choice not only serves her soul best, but it serves the Rav, our family, and the world best. This is the power of the Light. And this is the degree of self-knowledge and Light awareness that my mom has. It is truly amazing.

MY HOPE

My hope is that you—and all women—will recognize the Light that you carry within and know that your worth and value as a spiritual being is independent of any man—or any person, for that matter. If you had even the slightest notion of the strength and power that you walk around with every day, your doubts would vanish and your need for a man would dissolve. You would be left with the absolute certainty that you have everything you could possibly need, right here and right now. A desire to share your Light, your certainty, and your joy would overcome you. You would know that your desire to cultivate a relationship with a man has the primary purpose of bringing Light to your partner and loved ones—and to the entire world around you. When you have reached this level of consciousness, you will have reached (Heaven) the Light.

May each of you experience this reality.

THE KABBALAH CENTRE®

What is Kabbalah?

Kabbalah is the world's oldest body of spiritual wisdom, containing the long-hidden keys to the secrets of the Universe, as well as the keys to the mysteries of the human heart and soul. It's a workable system that allows you to understand your purpose for being here experiencing the joy you were put on Earth to have. In fact, that's what Kabbalah means—to receive, to get.

Kabbalah teaches that in order to claim the gifts you were created to receive, you need to earn them by undertaking your spiritual work—the process of fundamentally transforming yourself as you climb out of the darkness and into the Light. By helping you recognize the sources of negativity in your own mind and heart, Kabbalah gives you the tools for positive change.

Kabbalistic teachings explain the complexities of the material and the nonmaterial Universe and the physical and metaphysical nature of all humankind.

Moses, Pythagoras, and Sir Isaac Newton are a few of the individuals who studied Kabbalah to understand the spiritual laws of the Universe and their effect on the physical world.

Kabbalah is meant to be used, not merely learned. It can help you remove chaos, pain and suffering from your life and bring you clarity, understanding and freedom.

Who Can Study?

Today, millions of people of all faiths have discovered the wisdom and experienced the powerful effects of studying Kabbalah.

Why shouldn't they? Kabbalah works. When the wisdom and practical tools of Kabbalah are applied in life, positive experiences are the result. And Kabbalah can enhance the practice of any religion.

What Is The Kabbalah Centre®?

The Kabbalah Centre® is a spiritual organization dedicated to bringing the wisdom of Kabbalah to the world. The Kabbalah Centre® itself has existed for more than 80 years, but its spiritual lineage extends back to Rav Isaac Luria in the 16th century and even further back to Rav Shimon bar Yochai, who revealed the principal text of Kabbalah, the *Zohar*, more than 2,000 years ago.

The Kabbalah Centre® was founded in 1922 by Rav Yehuda Ashlag, one of the greatest kabbalists of the 20th Century. When Rav Ashlag left this world, leadership of The Kabbalah Centre® was taken on by Rav Yehuda Brandwein. Before his passing, Rav Brandwein designated Rav Berg as director of The Kabbalah Centre®. Now, for more than 30 years, The Centre has been under the direction of Rav Berg, his wife Karen Berg, and their sons, Yehuda Berg and Michael Berg.

Although there are many scholarly studies of Kabbalah, The Kabbalah Centre® does not teach Kabbalah as an academic discipline but as a way of creating a better life. The mission of The Kabbalah Centre® is to make the practical tools and spiritual teachings of Kabbalah available and accessible to everyone regardless of religion, ethnicity, gender or age.

The Kabbalah Centre® makes no promises. But if people are willing to work hard to grow and become actively sharing, caring and tolerant human beings, Kabbalah teaches that they will then experience fulfillment and joy in a way previously unknown to them. This sense of fulfillment, however, comes gradually and is always the result of the student's spiritual work.

Our ultimate goal is for all humanity to gain the happiness and fulfillment that is our true destiny.

Kabbalah teaches its students to question and test everything they learn. One of the most important teachings of Kabbalah is that there is no coercion in spirituality.

What Does The Kabbalah Centre® Offer?

Local Kabbalah Centres around the world offer onsite lectures, classes, study groups, holiday celebrations and services, and a community of teachers and fellow students. To find a Centre near you, go to www.kabbalah.com.

For those of you unable to access a physical Kabbalah Centre due to the constraints of location or time, we have other ways to participate in The Kabbalah Centre® community.

At www.kabbalah.com, we feature online blogs, newsletters, weekly wisdom, a store, and much more.

It's a wonderful way to stay tuned in and in touch, and it gives you access to programs that will expand your mind and challenge you to continue your spiritual work.

Student Support

The Kabbalah Centre® empowers people to take responsibility for their own lives. It's about the teachings, not the teachers. But on your journey to personal growth, things can be unclear and sometimes rocky, so it is helpful to have a coach or teacher. Simply call 1 800 KABBALAH toll free.

All Student Support instructors have studied Kabbalah under the direct supervision of Kabbalist Rav Berg, widely recognized as the preeminent kabbalist of our time.

We have also created opportunities for you to interact with other Student Support students through study groups, monthly connections, holiday retreats, and other events held around the country.

THE ZOHAR

Composed more than 2,000 years ago, the *Zohar* is a set of 23 books, a commentary on biblical and spiritual matters in the form of conversations among spiritual masters. But to describe the *Zohar* only in physical terms is greatly misleading. In truth, the *Zohar* is nothing less than a powerful tool for achieving the most important purposes of our lives. It was given to all humankind by the Creator to bring us protection, to connect us with the Creator's Light, and ultimately to fulfill our birthright of true spiritual transformation.

More than eighty years ago, when The Kabbalah Centre was founded, the *Zohar* had virtually disappeared from the world. Few people in the general population had ever heard of it. Whoever sought to read it—in any country, in any language, at any price—faced a long and futile search.

Today all this has changed. Through the work of The Kabbalah Centre and the editorial efforts of Michael Berg, the *Zohar* is now being brought to the world, not only in the original Aramaic language but also in English. The new English *Zohar* provides everything for connecting to this sacred text on all levels: the original Aramaic text for scanning; an English translation; and clear, concise commentary for study and learning.

The Living Kabbalah System™: Levels 1 & 2

Take Your Life to the Next Level™ with this step-by-step, 23-day system for transforming your life and achieving lasting fulfillment.

Created by Yehuda Berg and based on his belief that Kabbalah should be lived, not merely studied, this revolutionary interactive system incorporates the latest learning strategies, addressing all three learning styles:

- Auditory (recorded audio sessions)

- Visual (workbook with written concepts and graphics)

- Tactile (written exercises, self-assessments and physical tools)

The sturdy carrying case makes the system easy and convenient to use, in the car, at the gym, on a plane, wherever and whenever you choose. Learn from today's great Kabbalah leaders in an intimate, one-on-one learning atmosphere. You get practical, actionable tools and exercises to integrate the wisdom of Kabbalah into your daily life.

MORE BOOKS THAT CAN HELP YOU BRING THE WISDOM OF KABBALAH INTO YOUR LIFE

Kabbalah on Love
By Yehuda Berg

This charming little book has a simple yet profound message: Love is not something you learn or acquire but an essence within, waiting to be revealed. Buried by layers of ego, fear, shame, doubt, low self-esteem, and other limitations, the incredibly powerful force that is love can only be activated by sharing and serving unconditionally. Only then will the layers fall away and the essence of love reveal itself. The book draws the distinction between love and need, which is a selfish product of ego, and reminds us that we cannot love someone else until we figure out how to love ourselves and connect with the love within.

God Wears Lipstick: Kabbalah for Women
By Karen Berg

For thousands of years, women were banned from studying Kabbalah, the ancient source of wisdom that explains who we are and what our purpose is in this Universe. Karen Berg changed that. She opened the doors of The Kabbalah Centre to all who would seek to learn.

In *God Wears Lipstick*, Karen Berg shares the wisdom of Kabbalah, especially as it affects you and your relationships. She reveals a woman's special place in the Universe and why women have a spiritual advantage over men. She explains how to find your soul mate and your purpose in life, and empowers you to become a better human being.

The Secret: Unlocking the Source of Joy & Fulfillment
By Michael Berg

The Secret reveals the essence of life in its most concise and powerful form. Several years before the latest "Secret" phenomenon, Michael Berg shared the amazing truths of the world's oldest spiritual wisdom in this book. In it, he has pieced together an ancient puzzle to show that our common understanding of life's purpose is actually backwards, and that experiencing anything less than complete joy and fulfillment can be changed by correcting this misperception.

Rebooting: Defeating Depression with the Power of Kabbalah By Yehuda Berg

An estimated 18 million people in the United States suffer from depression—that's almost 10% of the population. So chances are good that you have, or someone you know has, been affected by it. Antidepressants, counseling, herbal remedies—all have been known to help treat the symptoms, but sometimes they fall short. If only you could click on the "Restart" button and get your internal software back on track. Now, in *Rebooting*, noted kabbalistic scholar and author Yehuda Berg shows how you can do just that by reconnecting with desire and light to emerge from this debilitating darkness.

Notes:

Notes:

Notes:

The *Spiritual* Rules of Engagement

Notes:

To everyone everywhere and every when,

especially those who are searching for their soul mate.

May we all receive and give as much Light as

we possibly can.